Workshop on Advances in Discourse Analysis and its Computational Aspects

(ADACA)

Held at the 24th International Conference on Computational Linguistics (COLING 2012)

Mumbai, India
15 December 2012

Editors:

Eva Hajičová
Lucie Poláková
Jiří Mírovský

ISBN: 978-1-62748-348-3

Printed from e-media with permission by:

Curran Associates, Inc.
57 Morehouse Lane
Red Hook, NY 12571

Some format issues inherent in the e-media version may also appear in this print version.

Printed by Curran Associates, Inc. (2013)

For permission requests, please contact the Association for Computational Linguistics at the address below.

Association for Computational Linguistics
209 N. Eighth Street
Stroudsburg, Pennsylvania 18360

Phone: 1-570-476-8006
Fax: 1-570-476-0860

acl@aclweb.org

Additional copies of this publication are available from:

Curran Associates, Inc.
57 Morehouse Lane
Red Hook, NY 12571 USA
Phone: 845-758-0400
Fax: 845-758-2634
Email: curran@proceedings.com
Web: www.proceedings.com

Preface

Discourse analysis as a domain focused on issues going beyond intra-sentential relations has been an important and intensively discussed topic of all prestigious linguistic and computational meetings, bringing important insights into the research area. Nevertheless we hope that our workshop on *Advances in Discourse Analysis and Its Computational Aspects* will not be just "one in the row" but will bring together and spread an up-to-date information on advanced computationally oriented studies in discourse analysis, and will provoke discussion on hot issues in the domain of the study in discourse, especially with respect to modern methodology and to computationally and corpus oriented research and its possible applications. Thus, we expect the workshop to attract a rather broad (and cross-domain) audience: those who are just starting their research in the given area will get enough stuff for thought how to proceed, and those who are in an advanced stage of their research will get a stimulating feedback from the floor and the discussion will make it possible for them to sharpen their ideas and plans.

In order to make these expectations real, the workshop program consists of two kinds of presentations: five invited position papers given by prominent researchers who have already had significant contributions to the field, and six papers selected during the anonymous review from those submitted by workshop participants. The topics of the position papers reflect the current state of the art and at the same time present a look ahead: *Aravind Joshi* (University of Pennsylvania, Philadelphia, USA), the founder and the head of the team which has offered the computational linguistic community one of the first comprehensive and most influential corpus of English annotated with discourse relations, the Penn Discourse TreeBank, opens a discussion on the specification of elements on which the annotation of discourse relations should rely, while *Nianwen (Bert) Xue* (Brandeis University, USA), who most unfortunately had at the last minute to cancel his personal attendance due to visa problems, in his abstract duly reminds us that a cross-lingual perspective introduces many not-yet or not-yet-fully explored phenomena that should be taken into account. *Kathleen McKeown* (Columbia University, New York, USA) documents that in language generation, discourse structure relations often play a prescriptive role in determining what to say next and she asks to which extent the annotation of the PDTB which couples discourse structure, syntactic structure and sense annotation offers an advantage over previous methods. *Kristiina Jokinen* (University of Helsinki, Finland and University of Tartu, Estonia) extends the discussion on information presentation to an interactive system with an important outreach to an application area. A non-negligible component part of the analysis and annotation of discourse relations is a cross-lingual computational study of anaphora accompanied by evaluation initiatives; the lessons learned during the experience with the annotation of the GNOME and ARRAU corpora of English, the LiveMemories corpus of Italian, and the ongoing annotation using the Phrase Detective game and the issues that still remain to be tackled – that is the subject of the position paper given by *Massimo Poesio* (University of Essex, Great Britain).

The timeline of the workshop program allows us to thematically group together the position papers with accepted presentations. We hope that such a grouping will help to concentrate on an intensive interaction and discussion of all the participants of the workshop. However, this does not mean that other relevant issues should be excluded from our discussion, both after the presentations and in the general discussion period at the end of the workshop.

Among the issues proposed to be discussed there are

- Intra-sentential and inter-sentential relations: commonalities and differences
- Explicit and implicit relations of coherence of discourse; means of implicit relations
- What can corpus annotation of discourse relations and related phenomena reveal?
- Annotation efforts undertaken in languages other than English, and their contribution to advances in Language Technologies and to a greater cross-linguistic understanding of coherence relations, their complexity and their lexicalization
- Advances in empirically-driven discourse-level methods of language processing (discourse parsing, sense detection) and their impact on theoretical understanding of discourse structure
- Discourse and dialogue, commonalities and differences (e.g. dialogue act standardization)
- Text segmentation and modeling of coherence in texts, tweets, dialogues, monologues etc.
- Structures other than coherence relations that discourse manifests (e.g. layout or "document structure"), or structure specific to particular genres (news report, scientific papers, errata, etc.)

We would like to thank all the invited speakers for their willingness to be with us at the workshop and to share their ideas with us, and also all the authors of the submissions for their contributions. We are most grateful to the Publication Chair Roger Evans for his most efficient efforts that helped us with the publication of the Workshop Proceedings and, last but not least, the local organizers of COLING 2012 for their continuous care of the COLING 2012 local organization for which they deserve a good measure of the credit.

Welcome to ADACA workshop at COLING 2012!

Eva Hajičová, Lucie Poláková, and Jiří Mírovský

ADACA organizers

Table of Contents

Workshop chairs:
Eva Hajičová, Lucie Poláková and Jiří Mírovský

Diamond sponsors

Tata Consultancy Services
Linguistic Data Consortium for Indian Languages (LDC-IL)

Gold Sponsors

Microsoft Research
Beijing Baidu Netcon Science Technology Co. Ltd.

Silver sponsors

IBM, India Private Limited
Crimson Interactive Pvt. Ltd.
Yahoo
Easy Transcription & Software Pvt. Ltd.

Workshop on Advances in Discourse Analysis and its Computational Aspects (ADACA)

Program

Saturday, 15 December 2012

10:00–10:20	Welcome, Introduction (Eva Hajičová)
10:20–11:00	*Remarks on some not so closed issues concerning discourse connectives (invited position paper)* Aravind Joshi
11:00–11:25	*Discourse Analysis of Sanskrit texts* Amba Kulkarni and Monali Das
11:25–12:00	Tea break
12:00–12:40	*Penn Discourse Treebank Relations and their Potential for Language Generation (invited position paper)* Kathleen McKeown
12:40–13:05	*Exploiting Discourse Relations between Sentences for Text Clustering* Nik Adilah Hanin Binti Zahri, Fumiyo Fukumoto and Suguru Matsuyoshi
13:05–13:30	*Measuring the Strength of Linguistic Cues for Discourse Relations* Fatemeh Torabi Asr and Vera Demberg
13:30–14:30	Lunch
14:30–15:10	*New Information in Wikitalk - story telling for information presentation (invited position paper)* Kristiina Jokinen
15:10–15:35	*Semi-Automatic Annotation of Intra-Sentential Discourse Relations in PDT* Pavlína Jínová, Jiří Mírovský and Lucie Poláková
15:35–16:00	*Incremental Construction of Robust but Deep Semantic Representations for Use in Responsive Dialogue Systems* Andreas Peldszus and David Schlangen
16:00–16:30	Tea break
16:30–17:10	*Empirical methods in the study of anaphora: lessons learned, remaining problems (invited position paper)* Massimo Poesio
17:10–18:00	General discussion: Where we are and where to go

Discourse Analysis of Sanskrit texts

Amba Kulkarni and Monali Das
Department of Sanskrit Studies, University of Hyderabad
apksh@uohyd.ernet.in, monactc.85@gmail.com

ABSTRACT
The last decade has seen rigorous activities in the field of Sanskrit computational linguistics pertaining to word level and sentence level analysis. In this paper we point out the need of special treatment for Sanskrit at discourse level owing to specific trends in Sanskrit in the production of its literature ranging over two millennia. We present a tagset for inter-sentential analysis followed by a brief account of discourse level relations accounting the sub-topic and topic level analysis, as discussed in the Indian literature illustrating an application of these to a text in the domain of vyākaraṇa (grammar).

KEYWORDS: Discourse analysis, Sanskrit, Saṅgati.

Proceedings of the Workshop on Advances in Discourse Analysis and its Computational Aspects (ADACA), pages 1–16,
COLING 2012, Mumbai, December 2012.

1 Introduction

Sanskrit, the classical language of India, has a huge collection of literature in almost all branches of knowledge – astronomy, mathematics, logic, philosophy, medicine, technology, dramatics, literature, poetics – to name a few. It was the medium of communications for all serious discourses and scholarly communications till recent times. This resulted in continuous production of literature in Sanskrit in various branches of knowledge systems of human endeavour for almost over 2 millennia. The total corpus of Sanskrit is almost 100 times those in Greek and Latin put together. However, the picture changed completely in the last two centuries. The traditional learning methods are replaced by the Western learning systems. As a consequence the knowledge in Sanskrit texts is inaccessible to the modern Indian scholars.

The main reasons behind the difficulty in accessing Sanskrit texts are:

- Sanskrit is influenced by the oral tradition, and hence the Sanskrit texts are continuous strings of characters without any punctuation marks or word or sentence boundaries. The characters at the juncture of boundary undergo euphonic changes making it difficult to 'guess' the boundaries.
- Sanskrit is very rich in morphology and is inflectional. This also makes it difficult to remember various inflections of a word, which differ with the last character of the word and its gender.
- Though a substantial vocabulary in modern Indian languages is from Sanskrit, there have been cases of meaning shifts, meaning expansion and meaning reduction. This makes it difficult for an Indian to understand the Sanskrit texts faithfully, unless he knows the original meaning of the words.
- Another important aspect is the presentation of texts. There are various trends in the Sanskrit literature. One of them is that of nested commentaries. The original text which is in a cryptic sūtra form, is commented upon by later scholars for more clarification. In order to clarify a content in this commentary another commentary would follow, and this continues leading to nested commentaries (see Appendix A for an example). Since the modern scholars are trained in modern learning methodologies they find it difficult to get familiar with the structure and decide the boundaries of various topics and sub topics, and thereby understand the texts.

1.1 Discourse Analysis in Indian Grammatical Tradition

The rich tradition of linguistics in India is more than two millennia old. Pāṇini's (around 500 B.C.) contribution to the grammar is as important a milestone in the development as that of Euclid in case of development of geometry in Europe (Staal, 1965). The discussions on the problem of meaning and the process of understanding the texts by philosophers like Bhartṛhari, Gaṅgeśa, and Kumārilabhaṭṭa resulted into three distinct schools of thought. With an aim to understanding the Vedas these schools developed the theories of verbal cognition - *Śābdabodha*. These schools differ mainly in the chief qualificand of the cognition, however more or less they agree on various other relations at gross level. These three schools are *Vyākaraṇa (Grammar), Nyāya (Logic) and Mīmāṁsā (Exegesis)*. Grammarians deal with the syntactic analysis to a considerable depth. Logicians and Mīmāṁsakas discuss various constraints such as *Akāṅkṣā (expectancy), Yogyatā (mutual compatibility) and Sannidhi (proximity)* to filter out nonsensical analysis. In his seminal attempt to describe the relation between word and its meaning, a logician Gadādhara (Śāstri, 1929) has provided the meanings of various pronouns and rules for tracing their antecedents. The Mīmāṁsakas further discuss various types of discourse relations called *Saṅgatis* for checking the consistency and coherence of the text. The coherence is tested at various levels viz.

(a) Śāstra saṅgati : The coherence at the level of the subject.

(b) Adhyāya saṅgati : The coherence at the level of a chapter or a book.

(c) Pāda saṅgati : The coherence at the level of a section.

(d) Adhikaraṇa saṅgati : The coherence at the level of a topic.

Each topic can further have one or more sub-topics, each sub-topic can have one or more paragraphs and a paragraph may consist of one or more sentences. Thus the topic level analysis involves following steps:

(i) Sentential analysis : Establishing relations among words in a sentence.

(ii) Paragraph level analysis : Identifying inter-sentential relations based on either explicit or implicit connectives.

(iii) Sub-topic level analysis : Establishing relations between the successive paragraphs showing the consistency of the argument leading to a sub-topic.

(iv) Topic level analysis : Topic level analysis shows the relevance of each sub-topic towards the goal of the main topic and thus the coherence.

1.2 Computational Discourse Analysis

With the emergence of computational linguistics, it is now possible to build tools which can assist a scholar in accessing Sanskrit texts, reducing his learning time. The Computational Linguistic tools are centered around the Western Linguistic theories and hence remain suited for English and other European Languages. Sanskrit is morphologically rich and is dominated by oral tradition. This results in Sanskrit text as a continuous string of characters, merging not only the word boundaries but sometimes the sentence boundaries as well. This therefore poses a big challenge to the computational processing of Sanskrit texts, requiring new innovative methods to handle segmentation taking into account euphonic changes effectively. As a result we see that much of the Sanskrit computational work is still at the level of word analysis and segmentation (Huet, 2009; Hellwig, 2009; Kumar et al., 2010). The rich inflectional morphology further makes the constituency parsers inappropriate for syntactic analysis of a sentence. While for positional languages such as English, the information of the relation between words is coded in positions and hence the constituent structures makes sense, for inflectionally rich languages like Sanskrit, the information of the relation is in the inflectional suffixes, which in turn allows for flexible word order, and thereby the dependency structure is more appropriate to represent the semantics expressed through the suffixes. A full fledged constraint parser using the concepts of Ākāṅkṣā (expectancy) and Sannidhi (proximity) has been developed by (Kulkarni et al., 2010). This parser handles some inter-sentential relations as well, and the work on anaphora resolution has just begun. Thus the work on discourse analysis for Sanskrit is yet in its infancy.

On the other hand we see major efforts at the level of discourse analysis in English and other European languages. Halliday and Hasan (1976) articulated the discourse theory and discussed about cohesion in discourse. Two main discourse structures were proposed viz. tree structure (Mann and Thompson, 1987) and graph (Wolf and Gibson, 2005). The prominent discourse theories are Rhetorical Structure Theory (RST), Linguistics Discourse Model (LDM), Discourse GraphBank (DG), and Discourse-Lexicalized Tree Adjoining Grammar (D-LTAG).

RST (Mann and Thompson, 1987) associates discourse relation with discourse structure. Here discourse units relate two adjacent units by discourse relations. In RST the proposed structure is a tree. Discourse structure is modelled by schemas where leaves are elementary discourse units – non-overlapping text spans and discourse relation holds between daughters of the same non-terminal node.

LDM (Polanyi, 1988) deals with discourse structure in the form of a tree. It differs from RST in distinguishing discourse structure from discourse interpretation. The discourse structure comes from the context free rules i.e. parent is interpreted as the interpretation of its children and the relationship between them.

In DG (Wolf and Gibson, 2005) discourse units are related to both adjacent and non-adjacent units. It was observed that crossing dependencies and nodes with multiple parents appear in texts vastly while RST does not allow these. In order to overcome these problems, graph representation was proposed by DG.

D-LTAG (Webber et al., 2001) builds on the observation that discourse connectives have both the syntactic as well as semantic function in the discourse. It considers discourse relations triggered by lexical elements. In D-LTAG, the predicates (verbs) are discourse connectives.

Webber and Joshi further proposed a tagset (Webber and Joshi, 2012) for annotating a corpus for discourse. This tagset is used to annotate the Penn Discourse Treebank. This tagset is neutral and does not make any assumptions about the form of the overall discourse structure of text. In addition to marking the arguments for both explicit as well as implicit connectives, it also marks senses and attribution of each discourse connective.

In the recent years there have also been efforts to deal with the coherence at the level of topic (Webber, 2006; Webber and Joshi, 2012).

All these computational models for discourse analysis are centered around English and other European languages. They are not appropriate to handle morphologically rich and more or less free word order language like Sanskrit with a special discourse structure of scientific and philosophical texts. Further, India has a strong grammatical tradition. So it is natural to look at this tradition for building computational models rather than trying to 'fit in' available models for Sanskrit.

In this paper we present a framework for discourse analysis in Sanskrit. The second section presents a brief report on the set of relations used for developing a Dependency Tree bank of Sanskrit corpus. The third section lists various inter-sentential relations for paragraph level analysis, discussed in Sanskrit literature. The fourth section provides a brief report on the *Saṅgatis* (relations) needed for analysing the inter-relations between paragraphs describing the same sub-topic. The fifth section lists the Saṅgatis used by the Indian logicians to establish the coherence and then we illustrate with an example how these Saṅgatis are useful for proper understanding of a text. Then we give a brief outline of three major trends in the production of scientific literature, and the current status of Sanskrit computational tools.

2 Sentence Level Analysis

In the traditional learning schools, the sentence level analysis is introduced at a tender age of 9 or 10 immediately after the students have memorized Śabdarūpa (noun-word forms), dhātupāṭha (verbal forms) and Amarakośa (a thesaurus). Then the students are taught one chapter of Raghuvaṃśa of Kālidāsa to imbibe in them the methodology of analysing the text. There are two prominant approaches viz Daṇḍānvaya (also known as anvayamukhī) and Khaṇḍānvaya (also known as kathambhūtinī). In the first aproach the teacher arranges all the words in prose order. In the second approach, on the other hand, the teacher gives the basic skeleton of a sentence and fills in other details by asking questions.[1] These questions are centered around the heads seeking their various modifiers. This later method of analysis is more close to the modern dependency parsing credited to (Tesnière, 1959). The dependency relations in Sanskrit have been proposed and thoroughly examined by the generations of scholars over a period of more than 2 millennia. Thus we are fortunate to have a well defined, time tested tagset for Sanskrit, unlike other languages such as English where special efforts were put in as described in PARC (King et al., 2003), Stanford dependency manual (M. Marneffe and Manning, 2006) etc. for defining the set of relations. Various relations described in the traditional grammar books have been compiled and classified by (Ramakrishnamacharyulu, 2009) under the two broad headings viz. inter- sentential and intra-sentential relations. This work provided a starting point for developing guidelines (Ramakrishnamacharyulu et al., 2011) for annotation of Sanskrit texts at kāraka (syntactico-semantic relations) level and also for the development of an automatic parser for Sanskrit. This tagset was further examined for the appropriateness of the granularity (Kulkarni and Ramakrishnamacharyulu, 2013). And a set of 31 relations were selected from among the 90 relations proposed in the original proposal. The reduction in the number of rules was to avoid the fine-grain distinction involving extra-linguistic knowledge. A constraint based parser[2] is developed to parse the Sanskrit sentences using these relations. A dependency tree bank of around 30K words is also annotated using this scheme.

3 Paragraph Level Analysis

The relations in the tag-set proposed by (Ramakrishnamacharyulu, 2009) contain intra-sentential relations as well. Some of the connectives connecting two sentences are single while most of them are parallel connectives or pairs. Each of these connectives takes two arguments. The relations are binary in nature except those indicated by the conjunctive and disjunctive particles. We follow the naiyāyikas (Indian Logicians) canonical form to represent the relations. In a sentence 'Rama sleeps', Rama is the agent of an activity of sleeping. This is represented as in Figure 1.

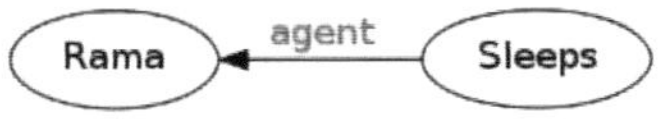

Figure 1: Convention for labelling relations

Note the direction of the arrowhead. This is interpreted as 'Rama' has an agent-hood conditioned/determined by an activity of sleeping.

In case of inter-sentential connectives, the two arguments, following logicians convention again,

[1]A very good illustration of these approaches is given in Tubb and Boose (2007).
[2]`http://sanskrit.uohyd.ernet.in/scl/SHMT/shmt.html`

are named by the general terms *anuyogika*[3] (combining) and *pratiyogī* (having a counter part). So, if C is the connective connecting two sentences S1 and S2 then the general structure is represented as in Figure 2.

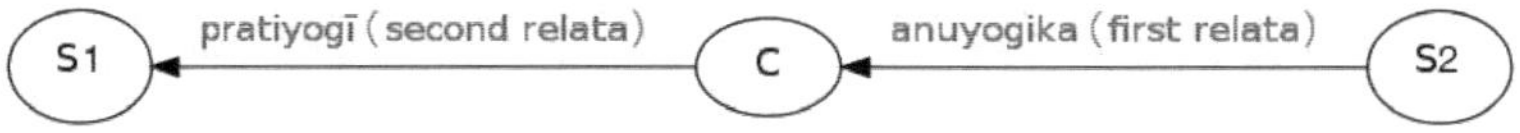

Figure 2: Discourse structure with single connective

When there are two parallel connectives C1 and C2 connecting S1 and S2 then the relation between them is represented as in Figure 3.

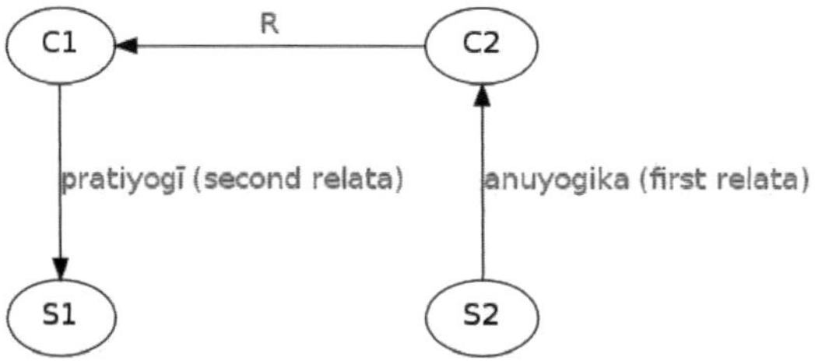

Figure 3: Discourse structure with paired connectives

Here R binds C1 and C2. The relation of the connectives with the sentence is through the main verbs. The sentences are further parsed as dependency trees. In case of paired connectives, we find instances of using either of the connectives or both. For example, in case of a paired connective 'yadi-tarhi' (if-then), we find instances of use of only 'yadi' (if), only 'tarhi' (then) and instances of both 'yadi-tarhi' (if-then). When only one of them is used in a sentence then the structure in Figure 3 collapses to that in Figure 2.

We present below various inter-sentential connectives in Sanskrit with an example for each. They are : yadi, tarhi, cet, tarhi-eva, yadyapi, tathāpi, athāpi, evamapi, yataḥ, tataḥ, yasmāt, tasmāt, ataḥ, atha, anantaram, api-ca, kiṁ-ca, kintu, parantu. We illustrate below one example of each type.

1. Cet (If/provided) [See Figure 4] :

Sanskrit	:	Tvam	icchasi	*cet*	aham	bhavataḥ	gṛham	āgamiṣyāmi.
Gloss	:	You	desire	provided	I	your	house	will_come.
English	:	Provided you desire I will come to your house.						

2. Yadi Tarhi (If-then) [See Figure 5] :

Sanskrit	:	*yadi*	bhavān	icchati	*tarhi*	aham	bhavataḥ	gṛham	āgamiṣyāmi.
Gloss	:	If	you	wish	then	I	your	house	will_come.
English	:	If you wish then I will come to your house.							

It is possible that this sentence may be written with either of the connectives viz. only *yadi* or only *tarhi*. In that case the parse structure will be similar to the one in figure 4.

For the remaining examples, only if the relations differ we present a diagram.

[3] S2 is the anuyogi. So if the arrowhead is pointing towards S2 the name of the relation would have been anuyogi. In this diagram, the arrowhead is pointing towards C, and hence the name of the relation is inverse of anuyogi, i.e. anuyogika.

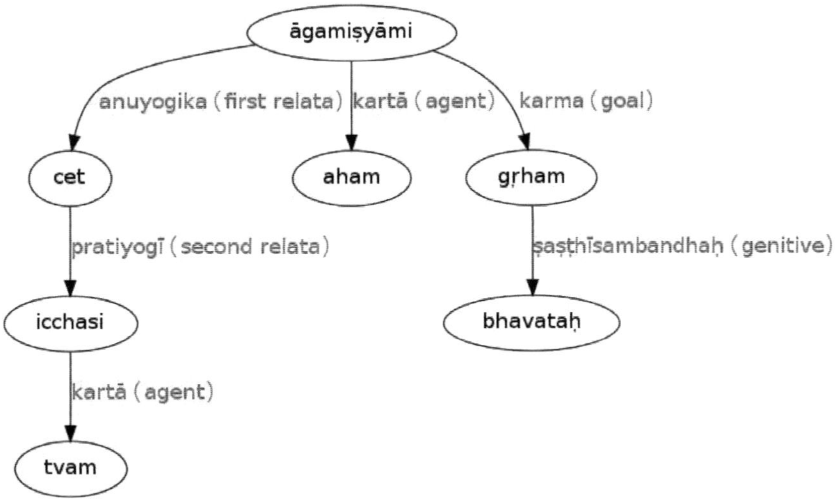

Figure 4: Cet

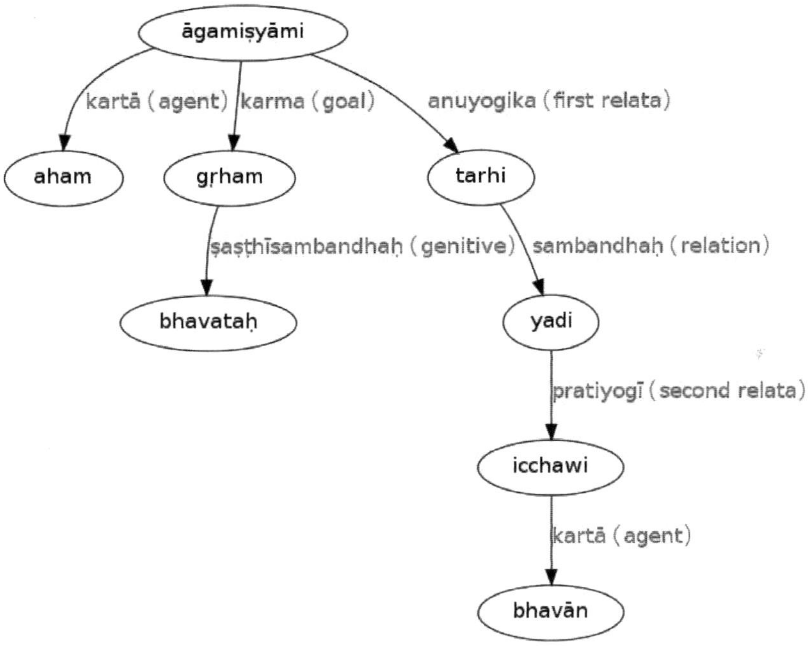

Figure 5: Yadi Tarhi

3. Yadyapi tathāpi (Even though, still):
   Sanskrit : *yadyapi* ayaṁ bahu prayāsaṁ kṛtavān *tathāpi* parīkṣāyām tu anuttīrṇaḥ.
   Gloss : Even-though he lot tried still examination failed.
   English : Even-though he tried very hard, still he failed in the examination.

4. Athāpi (Hence) :
   Sanskrit : parīkṣāyām aham anuttīrṇaḥ *athāpi* punaḥ likhiṣye.
   Gloss : in_examination I failed hence again will_write.
   English : I failed in the exam, hence I will attempt again.

5. Yataḥ, Tataḥ (Because-hence) :
Sanskrit : *yataḥ* ayam samaye na āgataḥ *tataḥ* parīkṣāyāṁ na anumataḥ.
Gloss: because he in_ time not came hence in_exam not permitted.
English:Because he did not arrive in time, he was not permitted to write the exam.

6. Ataḥ (Therefore) :
Sanskrit : ayam samaye na āgataḥ *ataḥ* parīkṣāyāṁ na anumataḥ.
Gloss : He in_time not came therefore in_exam not permitted.
English : He did not arrive in time therefore he was not permitted to write the exam.

7. Atha (Then) :
Sanskrit : prathamam ahaṁ śṛṇomi *atha* likhāmi.
Gloss : First I listen then write.
English : First I will listen and then will write.

8. Apica (And also) :
Sanskrit : bhikṣām aṭa *apica* gāṁ ānaya.
Gloss : alms ask and also cow bring.
English : Seek for alms and also bring cows.

9. Kintu/Parantu (But) :
Sanskrit : gajendraḥ tīvram prayatnam_akarot *kintu* nakra-grahāt na muktaḥ.
Gloss : gajendra lot tried but from_crocodile_jaw not escape.
English : Gajendra tried a lot but could not escape from the jaw of the crocodile.

10. Pūrvakālīkatvam (Preceding action):[see Figure 6]
Sanskrit uses a non-finite verb to indicate preceding action.
Sanskrit : rāmaḥ dugdhaṁ pītvā śālāṁ gacchati.
Gloss : rama milk after_drinking school goes.
English : Ram goes to school after drinking milk.

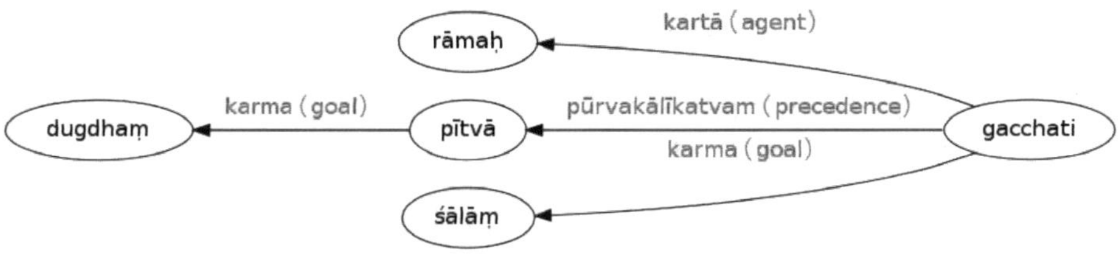

Figure 6: Pūrvakālīkatvam

11. Prayojanam (Purpose of the main activity) :[see Figure 7]
Sanskrit : aham bhavantaṁ mama gṛhe bhoktum āhvayāmi.
Gloss : I you my in_house to_have_food invite.
English : I invite you to my house for lunch/dinner.

12. Samānakālīkatvam (Simultaneity) :[see Figure 8]
Sanskrit : bālakaḥ jalam piban gacchati.
Gloss : boy water drinking goes.
English : The boy drinks water while going.

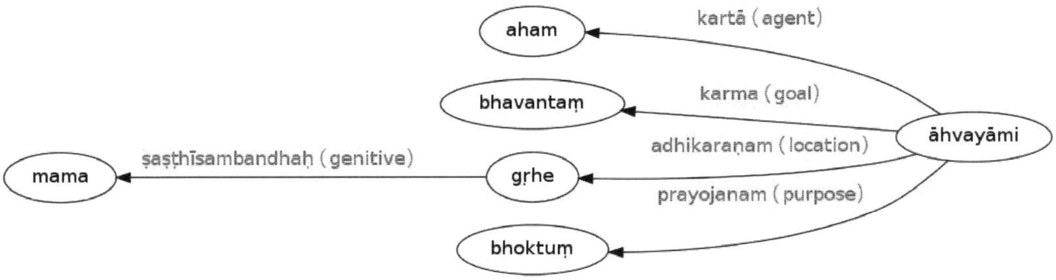

Figure 7: Prayojanam

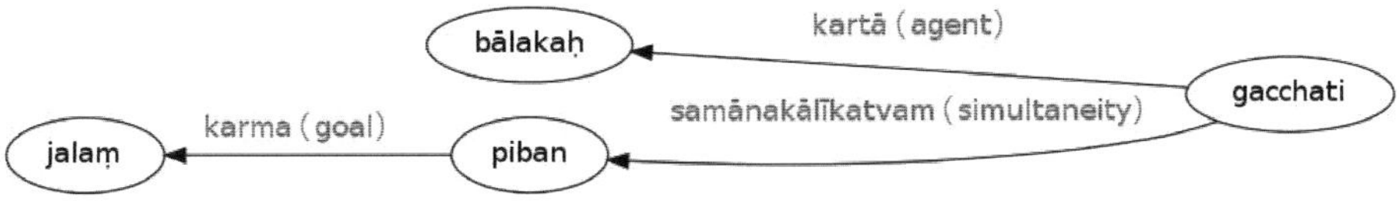

Figure 8: Samānakālīkatvam

In this tagging scheme we have neither deciphered the sense of the connectives nor did we decipher the relations expressed by the two arguments. In Ramakrishnamacharyulu 2009, these relations are classified further into 9 sub-headings as below.

1. Hetuhetumadbhāvaḥ (cause effect relationship) : yataḥ, tataḥ, yasmāt, tasmāt, ataḥ.
2. Asāphalyam (failure) : kintu.
3. Anantarakālīnatvam (following action) : atha.
4. Kāraṇasatve'api kāryābhāvaḥ / kāraṇābhāve'api kāryotpattiḥ (non-productive effort or product without cause) : yadyapi, tathāpi, athāpi.
5. Pratibandhaḥ (conditional) : yadi, tarhi, cet, tarhyeva.
6. Samuccayaḥ (conjunction) : ca, apica, kiñca.
7. Pūrvakālīkatvam : The non-finite verb form ending with suffix *ktvā* 'adverbial participial'.
8. Prayojanam (Purpose of the main activity) : The non-finite verb form ending with suffix *tumun* 'to-infinitive'.
9. Samānakālīkatvam (Simultaneity) : The non-finite verb form ending with suffix *Śatṛ and Śānac* 'present participle'.

In addition there are cases where the anaphora is used to indicate the simultaneity of events and the relation between events taking place in the same locus.

The analysis till this level is driven more by syntax and lexicon. The semantics is involved only to rule out incompatible parses.

4 Sub-Topic Level Analysis

Within each of the sub-topics, various paragraphs (each consisting of one or more sub-paragraphs) are connected by certain relations. The Mīmāmsakas (exegesists) discuss 6 inter-paragraph relations in the text *Jaiminīya Nyāyamālā Vistara by Mādhavācārya*. These relations are as follows.

1. Ākṣepa (Objection)
2. Dṛṣṭānta (Example)
3. Pratyudāharaṇa (Counter-example)
4. Prāsaṅgika (Corollary)
5. Upodghāta (Pre-requisite)
6. Apavāda (Exception)

These relations differ for different types of texts. For example, a commentary on Pāṇini's Aṣṭādhyāyī by Patañjali has a different structure. The dominant structure, as observed in the commentary on a sūtra 2.1.1 'samarthaḥ padavidhiḥ[4]' consists of the following relations.

1. Praśna – question
2. Ākṣepa – objection
3. Samādhāna – justification
4. Uttara – answer
5. Vyākhyā – elaboration

Appendix B gives a small snapshot of these relations. To a certain extent some of these relations such as Praśna, Ākṣepa and Samādhāna are identifiable with the lexical cues (Tātāchārya, 2005; Tubb and Boose, 2007). Since these relations are different for different sets of texts, it is necessary to compile these various sets before we develop any discourse analysis tagset.

5 Topic Level Analysis

Six relations among topics, called *Saṅgatis* are proposed in Indian tradition. They are (Śāstri, 1916):

1. Prasaṅga - Corollary.
2. Upodghāta - Pre-requisite.
3. Hetutā - Causal dependence.
4. Avasara - Provide an opportunity for further inquiry.
5. Nirvāhakaikya - The adjacent sections have a common end.
6. Kāryaikya - The adjacent sections are joint causal factors of a common effect.

[4]A compound is formed between the words which are mutually meaning-compatible.

5.1 Structure of Commentary on P2.1.1

Here we apply these *Saṅgatis* to reveal the underlying structure of a text in Grammar. The text selected is a commentary by patañjali on the sūtra *Samarthaḥ padavidhiḥ (2.1.1)* from Pāṇini's *Aṣṭādhyāyī*. The commentary consists of 213 paragraphs grouped into 14 topics as listed below.

(1) The meaning of the words in the sūtra explaining the derivational morphology.
Here only one word *vidhi* is discussed. The commentator did not find it necessary to comment on the other words.

(2) Type of sūtra.
The sūtras in Pāṇini's Aṣṭādhyāyī are classified into 6 types. Since it is not obvious from the sūtra to what type it belongs to, the commentator comments on its type and reasons thereof.

(3) Purpose of this rule with determined type.
These three steps have the common goal of explaining the sūtra at hand. After this, the commentator explains this sūtra systematically.

(4) Different characteristics of semantic connection (*samartha*).

(5) The first meaning of samartha viz. *ekārthībhāva* 'single integrated meaning' is examined.

(6) Various properties of single integrated meaning are examined.

(7) Meaning of *vṛtti* 'formation of new morphemes' giving single integrated meaning are dealt with.

(8) Possibility of the second meaning *vyapekṣā* of the word 'samartha' are ruled out.

(9) Definition of a sentence where *vyapekṣā* is prominent.

(10) Role of sāmarthya 'compatibility' in compound formation.

(11) Purpose behind the use of the second word *padavidhiḥ*.

(12) Objection that the sūtra is meaningless is refuted.

(13) Rules for compound formation following syntactic agreement are explained.

(14) Rules for deciding the gender and number of a compound.

These 14 topics are related to each other by one of the above 6 Saṅgatis. Figure 9 shows the relations among the topics.

6 Adhyāya Level Analysis

Among the scientific literature in Sanskrit we find three distinct trends. One is sūtra - bhāṣya - ṭīkā - ṭippaṇi popularly known as *Bhāṣya paramparā*. Here the original text is in the form of sūtras (cryptic aphorisms). This is followed by a commentary explaining the sūtras, optionally followed by an explanation (ṭīkā), a note (ṭippaṇi) etc. The commentaries may be nested, i.e. there is a commentary on the original sūtras and then commentary on this commentary, and further commentary on the sub-commentaries and so on. At each stage the number

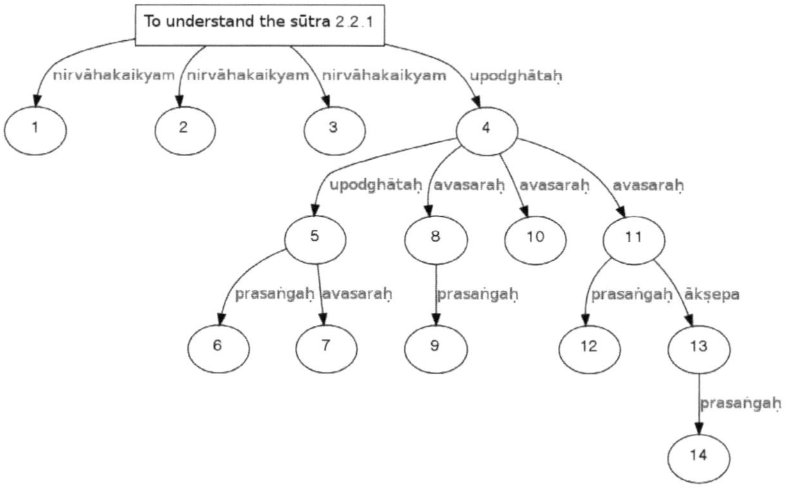

Figure 9: Discourse Structure of the commentary on "*Samarthaḥ Padavidhiḥ*"

of commentaries may be more than one. The sūtras as well as the commentaries and sub-commentaries follow a certain discourse structure.

Another trend is where the original text establishes a theory, and the later scholars write criticisms on it attacking the original view and proposing a new view. This trend is known as *khaṇḍana-maṇḍana paramparā*. And there can be a series of such texts criticizing the previous theory in the series and proposing a new theory. The structure of these texts then leads to a tree structure, where the siblings indicate different criticisms of the same text leading to different view points.

The third trend is to write *prakaraṇa granthas* (books dealing with a specific important topic among several topics discussed in the texts in sūtra form). These books are thus related to the original sūtra texts, but also have their own nested commentaries.

The grammar of these discourse structures then necessarily differ.

7 Towards Computability

In this paper we have described various level of analysis the tradition is following in order to understand the Sanskrit texts. Based on the available literature, a tagging scheme for dependency analysis and a dependency parser are developed. This parser is further enhanced to handle the anaphora and inter-sentential relations as well. Sanskrit has an advantage of having a huge corpus in the form of printed texts, with important literary works well analysed at various levels through commentaries. These works should be useful for further identifying the cues for establishing various saṅgatis. It is well known that different interpretations of the same text have resulted in different Indian philosophical schools. For interpretations we need an objective analysis of the text. We also need to have all possible interpretations presented in a nut-shell. With the help of computational tools now it is possible to explore all the possible interpretations of a given text at various stages of analysis systematically and present it in a concise form leaving the task of interpretation to the user. For example an expression 'naiṣadharājagatyā' from the 'Nalacaritam' (biography of Nala) has 6 different interpretations as described in the commentaries. The current tools help a student of Sanskrit to understand these various interpretations (Varalakshmi, 2013) in a systematic way. With the availability of a discourse level analysis, in future it should be then possible to understand how different interpretations emerge from the same text with different combinations of analysis at various stages.

References

Ganeri, J. and Miri, M. (2010). Sanskrit Philosophical Commentary. *Journal of The Indian Council of Philosophical Research*, Vol. 27:187–207.

Hellwig, O. (2009). Extracting Dependency Trees from Sanskrit Texts. In Kulkarni, A. and Huet, G., editors, *Proceedings, Third International Sanskrit Computational Linguistics Symposium*, pages 106–115. Springer-Verlag, LNAI 5406.

Huet, G. (2009). Formal structure of Sanskrit text: Requirements analysis for a mechanical Sanskrit processor. In Huet, G., Kulkarni, A., and Scharf, P., editors, *Sanskrit Computational Linguistics 1 & 2*. Springer-Verlag, LNAI 5402.

Joshi, S. D. (1968). *Patañjali's Vyākaraṇa Mahābhāṣya Samarthāhnika (P 2.1.1) Edited with Translation and Explanatory Notes*. Center of Advanced Study in Sanskrit, Poona, first edition.

King, T. H., Crouch, R., Riezler, S., Dalrymple, M., and Kaplan, R. (2003). The PARC 700 dependency bank. In *Proceedings of the Fourth International Workshop on Linguistically Interpreted Corpora (LINC-03)*.

Kulkarni, A., Pokar, S., and Shukl, D. (2010). Designing a Constraint Based Parser for Sanskrit. In Jha, G. N., editor, *Proceedings, Fourth International Sanskrit Computational Linguistics Symposium*, pages 70–90. Springer-Verlag, LNAI 6465.

Kulkarni, A. and Ramakrishnamacharyulu, K. V. (2013). Parsing Sanskrit Texts : Some Relation Specific Issues. In *Proceedings, Fifth Sanskrit Computational Linguistics Symposium*. D. K. Publisher.

Kulkarni, A., Shukl, D., and Pokar, S. (2012). Mathematical Modeling of Ākāṅkṣā and Sannidhi for Parsing Sanskrit. 15th World Sanskrit Conference, Delhi.

Kumar, A., Mittal, V., and Kulkarni, A. (2010). Sanskrit compound processor. In Jha, G. N., editor, *Proceedings, Fourth International Sanskrit Computational Linguistics Symposium*. Springer-Verlag, LNAI 6465.

M. Marneffe, B. M. and Manning, C. D. (2006). Generating typed dependency parses from phrase structure parses. In *The fifth international conference on Language Resources and Evaluation, LREC 2006, Italy*.

Mann, W. C. and Thompson, S. A. (1987). *Rhetorical Structure Theory : A Theory of Text Organization (Reprinted from The Structure of Discourse)*. ISI Reprint series 87–190.

Polanyi, L. (1988). A formal model of discourse structure. *Journal of Pragmatics*, 12:601–638.

Prasad, R., Miltsakaki, E., Dinesh, N., Lee, A., Joshi, A., Robaldo, L., and Webber, B. (2007). *The Penn Discourse Treebank 2.0 Annotation Manual*.

Ramakrishnamacharyulu, K. V. (2009). Annotating Sanskrit Texts Based on Sābdabodha Systems. In Kulkarni, A. and Huet, G., editors, *Proceedings, Third International Sanskrit Computational Linguistics Symposium*, pages 26–39. Springer-Verlag, LNAI 5406.

Ramakrishnamacharyulu, K. V., Pokar, S., Shukl, D., and Kulkarni, A. (2011). *Annotation Scheme for Kaaraka level tagging and guidelines*.

Śāstri, A. (1916). *Kārikāvalī with the commentaries Muktāvalī, Dinakarī, Rāmarudrī (edited with footnotes by Ananta Śāstri), page 286–287*. Nirṇaya Sāgara Press, Bombay.

Śāstri, G. D. (1929). *Śaktivāda with Vivṛti commentary by Harinātha Tarka Siddhānta Bhaṭṭāchārya, edited with critical notes*. Chowkhamba Sanskrit Series Office, Benares.

Śrī Jīvānanda Vidyāsāgar Bhaṭṭācārya (1989). *Śrī Mādhavācāryaviracita Jaiminīya Nyāyamālāvistaraḥ*. Kṛṣṇadās Academy, Varanasi.

Staal, F. (1965). Euclid and Paṇini. *Philosophy of East and West*, 15:99–116.

Tātāchārya, N. S. R. (2005). *Śābdabodhamīmāṃsā: The sentence and its significance Part-I to V*. Institute of Pondicherry and Rashtriya Sanskrit Sansthan, New Delhi.

Tesnière, L., editor (1959). *Éléments de Syntaxe Structurale*. Klincksieck, Paris.

Tubb, G. A. and Boose, E. R. (2007). *Scholastic Sanskrit: A Manual for Students*. Columbia University, New York.

Varalakshmi, K. (2013). Śleṣa Alaṅkāra - A Challenge for Testing Sanskrit Analytical Tools. In *Proceedings, Fifth Sanskrit Computational Linguistics Symposium*. D. K. Publisher.

Webber, B. (2006). Accounting For Discourse Relations : Constituency and Dependency. *Festschrift for Ron Kaplan*.

Webber, B. and Joshi, A. (2012). Discourse Structure and Computation : Past, Present and Future. In *Proceedings of the ACL-2012 Special Workshop on Rediscovering 50 Years of Discoveries*.

Webber, B., Joshi, A., Sarkar, A., Prasad, R., Miltsakaki, E., and Forbes, K. (2001). D-LTAG System - Discourse Parsing with a Lexicalized Tree Adjoining Grammar. In Kruijff-Korbayová, I. and Steedman, M., editors, *Workshop on Information Structure, Discourse Structure and Discourse Semantics*.

Wolf, F. and Gibson, E. (2005). Representing discourse coherence: a corpus-based study. *Computational Linguistics*, 31:249–287.

A Nested Commentaries

This is an introductory section of a prakaraṇa grantha *Vaiyākaraṇa-siddhānta-laghu-mañjūṣā* with a commentary Ratnaprabhā by Sabhāpati Upādhyāya.
We show below the original text, followed by the commentary, as it appears in the printed text.

Original : tatra vākyasphoṭo mukhyo loke tasyaivārthabodhakatvāttenaivārthasamāpteśca,
gloss : There, the process of understanding the meaning of a sentence is primary. This process has the property of conveying the meaning and therefore it itself leads to the completion of meaning.
Commentary : tatreti nirdhāraṇe saptamī, tathā ca siddhāntaghaṭakovākyasphoṭo mukhya ityarthaḥ. *bodhakatvāditi – yadyapyāntarasphoṭasyaiva vācakatvasya siddhāntayiṣyamāṇatayā

vāhyasya padasamūharūpavākyasya na vācakatvaṃ tathāpi tattādātmyāpannatvena tasyāpi tattvaṃ bodhyam. *tenaiva – vākyenaiva. *arthasamāpteriti vākyasyaiva nirākāṅkṣārthabodhakatvenārthasya pūrṇatvānnirākāṅkṣatvāditi yāvat.

If this piece is presented in this way, it is difficult to follow the commentary. We present below the original text segmented and commentary split into several footnotes placed at relevant places.

Segmented : tatra[5] vākyasphoṭaḥ mukhyaḥ loke tasya eva artha bodhakatvāt[6] tena eva[7] artha samāpteḥ ca,[8]

We observe that this makes it easy to read and understand the texts, since now we can 'see' the underlying structure. But we cannot use this technique further since nesting of footnotes after a certain limit becomes unwieldy. The current hyper text technology however makes it easy to present this text in the form of hyper text with links, allowing a smooth representation of the nested commentaries.

B Original text of Mahābhāṣya with relations among the paragraphs

This is the 4th sub-topic from the commentary by Patañjali on P2.1.1. The relations are marked manually, originally in the Nirṇaya sāgara edition of the mahābhāṣya which was further enhanced by Joshi in his edition (Joshi, 1968). The numbers indicate the serial number of paragraphs from the beginning of the commentary on P2.1.1.

Sub-Topic starts: *atha sāmarthyalakṣaṇabhedanirūpaṇādhikaraṇam*
(Now starts the section in which the different characteristic of semantic connection are examined.)

Relation: *praśnabhāṣyam* (question)
41. *atha kriyamāṇe'api samarthagrahaṇe samarthamityucyate kiṃ samarthaṃ nāma* |
(Now, apart from the question whether (the word) *samartha* should be mentioned in P. 2.1.1 (or not), (when) you say *samartha*, what do you really mean by *samartha*?)

Relation: *samādhānavārttikam* (justification)
Vārttika: pṛthagarthānāmekārthībhāvaḥ samarthavacanam ||1 ||
(The word *samartha* (means) single integrated meaning of words which (when uncompounded) have separate meanings (of their own).)

Relation: *vyākhyābhāṣyam* (elaboration)
42. *pṛthagarthānām padānāmekārthībhāvaḥ samarthamityucyate* |
((When) we say *samartha*, (it means) single integrated meaning of words which (when uncompounded) have separate meanings (of their own).)

---

[5]tatreti nirdhāraṇe saptamī, tathā ca siddhāntaghaṭakovākyasphoṭo mukhya ityarthaḥ.

[6]bodhakatvāditi – yadyapyāntarasphoṭasyaiva vācakatvasya siddhāntayiṣyamāṇatayā vāhyasya padasamūharūpavākyasya na vācakatvaṃ tathāpi tattādātmyāpannatvena tasyāpi tattvaṃ bodhyam.

[7]tenaiva – vākyenaiva.

[8]arthasamāpteriti vākyasyaiva nirākāṅkṣārthabodhakatvenārthasya pūrṇatvānnirākāṅkṣatvāditi yāvat.

Relation: *praśnabhāṣyam* (question)
43. *kva punaḥ pṛthagarthāni kvaikārthāni* |
(But where (do words) have separate meanings (of their own), (and) where (do they) have a single meaning?)

Relation: *uttarabhāṣyam* (answer)
44. *vākye pṛthagarthāni/rājñaḥ puruṣa iti/samāse punarekārthāni rājapuruṣa iti* |
(In the uncompounded word group (words) have separate meaning (of their own), like in *rājñaḥ puruṣaḥ*: 'king's man'. But in a compound, (words) have a single meaning, like *rājapuruṣaḥ*: 'king-man'.)

Relation: *ākṣepabhāṣyam* (objection)
45. *kimucyate pṛthagarthānīti yāvatā rājñaḥ puruṣa ānīyatāmityukte rājapuruṣa ānīyate rājapuruṣa iti ca sa eva* |
(What do you say: '(words) having separate meanings (of their own)'? Because when we say: 'let the king's man be brought', the king-man is brought. And (when we say): '(let) the king-man (be brought)', the same (man is brought).)

Relation: *samādhānabhāṣyam* (justification)
46. *nāpi brūmo'anyasyānayanaṃ bhavatīti*|
(We do not say at all that a different person is brought.)

Sub-topic ends: *iti sāmarthyalakṣaṇabhedanirūpaṇādhikaraṇam*
(Here ends the section in which the different characteristics of semantic connection are examined.)

Exploiting Discourse Relations between Sentences for Text Clustering

*Nik Adilah Hanin Zahri**
Fumiyo Fukumoto
Suguru Matsuyoshi
Interdisciplinary Graduate School of Medicine and Engineering,
University of Yamanashi, Japan
`g09dh103*,fukumoto,sugurum@yamanashi.ac.jp`

ABSTRACT

Over the years, the usage of discourse relations has been proven to enhance many applications such as text summarization, question answering and natural language generation. This paper proposes an approach that expands the benefit of discourse relations for natural language processing from a different aspect. We exploit the discourse relations existing between sentences to generate clusters of similar sentences from document sets. We first examined and defined the type of discourse relations that useful to retrieve sentences with identical content. We then assigned these relations to each sentence pair using a machine learning method. Finally we performed discourse relation-based clustering algorithm to generate clusters of similar sentences. We evaluated our method by measuring the cohesion and separation of the clusters and compared to a well recognized clustering method. The experimental result shows that our method performed significantly well, which demonstrated that discourse relation between sentences can be exploited for text clustering.

KEYWORDS : discourse relation, rhetorical relation, text clustering, SVMs, cluster validation

Proceedings of the Workshop on Advances in Discourse Analysis and its Computational Aspects (ADACA), pages 17–32,
COLING 2012, Mumbai, December 2012.

1 Introduction

The massive amount of data growth each day has become motivation for many researchers to develop text processing system with the ability to comprehend and process data effectively. The interpretation of how the phrases, clauses, and texts relate to each other is crucial to retrieve relevant information from texts. Therefore, the knowledge of discourse relation is prominent for natural language processing.

Many discourse coherent structures have been proposed over the years, such as Rhetorical Structure Theory (RST) (Mann and Thompson, 1987), RST Treebank (Carlson *et al.*, 2002), Lexicalized Tree-Adjoining Grammar based discourse (Webber *et al.*, 2003), Cross-document Structure Theory (CST) (Radev *et al.*, 2004), and Discourse GraphBank (Wolf and Gibson, 2005, 2006). Discourse GraphBank represents discourse relation as graph structure, while other works represent them as hierarchical structure between textual units. Each work proposed different kind of methods to distinguish how events in text are related by identifying the transition point of a relation from one text span to another. Here, similar to the TDT project, an event refers to something that occurs at a specific place and time associated with some specific actions. This gives system abilities to detect important information or content within the text spans. For instance, the following example describes "*Evidence*" relation between texts proposed by RST.

Example 1:
S_1: Smokes billows from the Pirelli building.
S_2: The Pirelli Building in Milan, Italy, was hit by a small plane.

S1 describes an event (claim), while *S2* describes the information to increase the reader's belief, which is the evidence of why the event occurred. This relation indicates that information in *S2* is necessary for *S1* to take place. Consider another example of discourse relation from different structure. The following sentences describe "*Subsumption*" relation defined by CST.

Example 2:
S_3: Police were trying to keep people away, and many ambulances were at the scene.
S_4: Police and ambulance were at the scene.

CST defined sentences with *Subsumption* relation as having the same content along with additional facts in one sentence compared to another. From this example, *Subsumption* indicates that the content conveyed by *S4* is alternatively can be expressed in *S3* with more information.

We found that discourse relation between sentences not only indicates how two sentences are connected to each other, but also shows the amount of similar contents in both sentences. Relations such as *Identical* (defined in many discourse structures), *Subsumption* (CST), and *Generalization* (RST), links two text span in different way, however, provides identical information regarding the corresponding event. For instance, we observed that the same information can be extracted from *Subsumption* in *Example 2*, where both sentences indicate that police and ambulance were at the scene.

Therefore, we are motivated to explore the potential of discourse relation further more. By exploiting discourse relation between text spans, we believe that clusters of similar sentences can be constructed. We propose a method that establishes the benefit of discourse relation in generating cluster of similar sentences. Our main objective is to expand the usage of discourse relation to data mining in natural language processing. In addition, we also hope to explore the construction of text clustering based on user preference, where users can determine how much similarity of information allowed in a text cluster according to the type of discourse relations used during clustering, which is difficult to achieve only with lexical and syntactic features of the sentences. For instance, clustering of sentences with *Identity* relation would only allow sentences with the exact same information within a cluster, while sentences with *Overlap* would include sentences with partial overlapping information within a cluster.

Our method consists of three main steps. We first define discourse relations which are useful for text clustering. Then, we identify these relations using Support Vector Machine (SVMs) (Vapnik, 1995). Finally, we performed a discourse relation based clustering algorithm to create clusters of similar sentences. Next section provides an overview of the existing works regarding discourse relation. Section 3 describes the framework of our system. In Section 4, we report experimental results and conclude our discussion with some direction for further works.

2 Previous Work

Since large scale machine readable textual corpus has become available, many techniques have been proposed to harvest vital information from documents using discourse relations analysis. Up until now, discourse relations have benefit various NLP applications such as text summarization ((Marcu, 1997), (Zhang *et al.*, 2002), (Radev *et al.*, 2004), (Uzêda *et al.*, 2009), (Louis *et al.*, 2012)), question answering ((Litkowski, 2002), (Verbe and Oostdijk, 2007)) and natural language generation ((Theune, 2002), (Piwek *et al.*, 2010)).

In text summarization, discourse relations are used to produce optimum ordering of sentences in a document, and remove redundancy from generated summaries. One of the well known works is CST based text summarization (Zhang *et al.*, 2002). In this work, sentences with most relations in the documents are considered to be important. They proposed an enhancement of text summarization by replacing low-salience sentences with sentences having maximum numbers of CST relations. Another work, (Uzêda *et al.*, 2009) presents comparative evaluation of RST-based text summarization methods. Besides informativeness, they also examined the effect of summary characteristics such as coherence and cohesion against each RST methods. One of the most recent work is a deep knowledge summarizer system (Jorge, 2010), which ranks input sentences according to the number of CST relations existing between sentences in accordance with user preference. They also demonstrated the effectiveness of redundancy elimination in summary using discourse relations. Most of the CST-based work observed the effects of individual CST relationships to the summary generation, and focused on the user preference based summarization, which requires manually annotated corpus.

The relevance of discourse analysis in QA application is pointed out by (Litkowski, 2002). This approach makes use of structural information of sentences, *e.g.*, discourse entities, semantic relation to generate database for question answering system. Another work, (Verbene *et al.*, 2007) suggested that the propositions of a question topic and answer are both represented by a text span in document, where the connection between text spans are described by RST relation. The topic of text span that matches RST tree will be the answer to the wh*y*-question.

Many of the previous works mentioned in the above show that the information obtained by discourse relation can improve single or multi-document summarization and QA application. In contrast, our work has different objective and approach. We investigated the potential of discourse relation in retrieving similar sentences, *i.e.* text clustering for data mining.

3 Framework

3.1 Redefinition of Discourse Relations

Different work proposed different types and definitions of discourse relations. Since our objective is to retrieve sentences with similar content using discourse relation, discourse structure that defines discourse relation between two text spans is mostly appropriate. Therefore, in this paper, we adopted the definition of rhetorical relation by CST (Radev *et al.*, 2004). We examined the definition of 18 types of CST relations in order to select relevant rhetorical relations for this work. According to the definition by CST, some of the relationship presents similar surface characteristics. Except for different version of event description, relations such as *Paraphrase, Modality* and *Attribution* share similar characteristic of information content with *Identity*. Consider the following example:

Example 3:
S_5: *RAI state TV reported that the pilot said the SOS was because of engine trouble.*
S_6: *RAI state TV reported that the pilot said he was experiencing engine trouble.*

Both sentences demonstrate an example of sentence pair that can represent *Identity, Paraphrase, Modality* and *Attribution* relations. The quality and amount of the information in both sentences are the same. Another example of sentence pair that can represent similar relations is shown in the following example:

Example 4:
S_7: *The crash put a hole in the 25th floor of the Pirelli building, and smoke was seen pouring from the opening.*
S_8: *A small plane crashed into the 25th floor of a skyscraper in downtown Milan today.*

Both sentences can be categorized as *Elaboration* and *Follow-up*. We can see from *Example 5* that *Subsumption* and *Elaboration* also shares some similar characteristics.

Example 5:
S_9: *The building houses government offices and is next to the city's central train station.*
S_{10}: *The building houses the regional government offices, authorities said.*

Thus, sentence pair connected as *Subsumption* can also be defined as *Elaboration*. However, sentence pair belongs to *Elaboration* in *Example 2* cannot be defined as *Subsumption*. Here, *Subsumption* denotes S_2 as the subset of S_1, but as for *Elaboration*, S_2 is not necessary a subset of S_1. Therefore, we keep *Subsumption* and *Elaboration* as two different relations so that we can precisely perform the automated identification of discourse relation by using SVMs.

We redefined the definition of relations from CST by combining the relations types that resemble each other as described in *Example 3*, *4* and *5*. *Fulfillment* by CST refers to sentence pair which asserts the occurrence of predicted event, where overlapped information present in both sentences. Therefore, we combined *Fulfillment* and *Overlap* as one type of relation. As for *Change of Perspective, Contradiction* and *Reader Profile*, these relations generally refer to sentence pairs presenting different information regarding the same subject. Thus, we simply merged these relations as one group. We also combined *Description* and *Historical Background*, as both type of relations provide description (historical or present) of an event. The combination of rhetorical relations in this paper is concluded in Table 1. We modified the definition of each relation in accordance with the combination of relations shown in Table 1. The taxonomy for rhetorical relations we used in the system is described in Table 2. By definition, although *Change of Topics*

Relations by CST	Relations by System
Identity, Paraphrase, Modality, Attribution	Identity
Subsumption, Indirect Speech, Citation	Subsumption
Elaboration, Follow-up	Elaboration
Overlap, Fulfillment	Overlap
Change of Perspective, Contradiction, Reader Profile	Change of Topics
Description, Historical Background,	Description
Translation, Summary	-
-	No Relations

TABLE 1 – Combination of CST relations

Relations	Definition
Identity	S_1 and S_2 contain the same information
Subsumption	S_1 contains all information in S_2, plus other additional information not in S_2
Elaboration	S_1 elaborates or provide more information given generally in S_2.
Overlap	S_1 and S_2 provides partial overlapping information
Change of Topics	S_1 and S_2 provide different facts about the same entity.
Description	S_1 gives historical or present description about any entity mentioned in S_2.
No Relations	No relation exits between S_1 and S_2.

TABLE 2 – Redefinition of discourse relations

and *Description* does not accommodate the purpose of text clustering, we still included these relations for evaluation. We also added *No Relation* to the type of relations used in this work. We combined the 18 types of relations by CST into 7 types, which we assumed that it is enough to evaluate the potential of discourse relation in text clustering.

3.2 Determining Discourse Relations Using SVMs

To identify discourse relations, we used a machine learning approach, Support Vector Machine (SVMs) (Vapnik, 1995). We used CST-annotated sentences pair obtained from CST Bank (Radev *et al.*, 2004) as training data for the SVMs. Each data is classified into one of two classes, where we defined the value of the features to be 0 or 1. Features with more than 2 value will be normalized into [0,1] range. This value will be represented by 10 dimensional space of a 2 value vector, where the value will be divided into 10 value range of [0.0,0.1], [0.1,0.2], …, [0.9,1.0]. For example, if the feature of text span S_j is 0.45, the surface features vector will be set into 0001000000. We extracted 2 types of surface characteristic from both sentences, which are lexical similarity between sentences and the sentence properties. Although the similarity of information between sentences can be determined only with lexical similarity, we also included sentences properties as features to emphasis which sentences provide specific information, *e.g.* location and time of the event. We provided the surface characteristics to SVMs for learning and classification of the text span S_1 according to the given text span S_2.

3.2.1 Lexical Similarity between Sentences

The amount of overlapping information among sentences is important to determine the type of discourse relations exist between them. Here, we used a few similarity measurements to compute the similarity between word content in both sentences from different aspects. We defined nouns, verbs and adjectives as word content in the experiment.

1. Cosine Similarity

   We compute the similarity of both sentences using cosine similarity measurement, defined as follows:

   $$\cos(S_1, S_2) = \frac{\sum s_{1,i} * s_{2,i}}{\sqrt{\sum (s_{1,i})^2} * \sqrt{\sum (s_{2,i})^2}} \quad (1)$$

   where S_1 and S_2 represents the frequency vector of the sentence pair, S_1 and S_2, respectively. The cosine similarity metric measures the correlation between the two sentences. We observed the following 5 types of similarity in this experiment:

   i) Similarity between word contents
   ii) Similarity of *nouns* tokens
   iii) Similarity of *verbs* tokens
   iv) Similarity of *adjectives* tokens
   v) Similarity of bigram words

   We not only measure the similarity value of words, but also consider the similarity value of word sequence in (v). We found that different word sequence sometimes provides different meaning. For example, the word "*test driving*" and "*driving test*". The word "*test driving*" refers to the action of driving a vehicle in order to evaluate its performance, meanwhile "*driving test*" refers to procedure designed to test a person's ability to drive a motor vehicle. The words ordering indirectly determine the semantic meaning in sentences. Therefore, we included the similarity of bigram words in the measurement.

2. Overlap ratio of words from S_1 in S_2 , and vice versa

   The overlap ratio is measured to identify whether all the words in S_2 are also appear in S_1, and vice versa. This measurement will determine how much the sentences match with each other. For instance, given the sentences pair with relations of *Subsumption,* the ratio of words from S_2 appear in S_1 will be higher than the ratio of words from S_1 appear in S_s. We add this measurement because cosine similarity does not extract this characteristic from sentences. The overlap ratio is measured as follows:

   $$wol(S_1) = \frac{\#commonwords(S_1, S_2)}{\#words(S_1)} \times 2 \quad (2)$$

   $$wol(S_2) = \frac{\#commonwords(S_1, S_2)}{\#words(S_2)} \times 2 \quad (3)$$

   where "*#commonword*" and "*#words*" represent the number of matching words and the number of words in a sentence, respectively. The feature with higher overlap ratio is set to 1, and 0 for lower value.

3. Longest Common Substring

Longest Common Substring metric extracts the maximum length of matching word sequence against S_1, given two text span, S_1 and S_2 .

$$lcs(S_1) = \frac{Length(MaxComSubstring(S_1, S_2))}{Length(S_1)} \tag{4}$$

The metric value shows if both sentences are using the same phrase or term, which will benefit the identification of *Overlap* or *Subsumption*.

4. Ratio overlap of grammatical relationship for S_1

We used a broad-coverage parser of English language, MINIPAR (Lin, 1994) to parse S_1 and S_2, and extract the grammatical relationship between words in the text span. Here we extracted the number of *surface subject* and the *subject of verb* (*subject*) and *object of verbs* (*object*). We then compared the grammatical relationship in S_1 which occur in S_2, compute as follows:

$$Subj\_ove(S_1) = \frac{\#comSubj(S_1, S_2)}{\#Subj(S_1)} \tag{5}$$

$$Obj\_ove(S_1) = \frac{\#comObj(S_1, S_2)}{\#Obj(S_1)} \tag{6}$$

The ratio value describes whether S_2 provides information regarding the same entity of S_1 , *i.e. Change of Topics*. We also compared the *subject* in S_1 with *noun* of S_2 to examine if S_1 is discussing topics about S_2.

$$SubjNoun\_ove(S_1) = \frac{\#com\ Subj(S_1)Noun(S_2)}{\#Subj(S_1)} \tag{7}$$

The ratio value will show if S_1 is describing information regarding subject mention in S_2, *i.e. Description*.

3.2.2 Sentences Properties

The type of information described in two text spans is also crucial to classify the type of discourse relation. Thus, we extracted the following information as additional features for each relation.

1. Number of entities

Sentences describing an event often offer information such as the place where the event occurs (location), the party involves (person, organization or subject), or when the event takes place (time and date). The occurrences of such entities can indicate how informative the sentence can be, thus can enhance the classification of relation between sentences. Therefore, we derived these entities from sentences, and compared the number of entities between them.

We used Information Stanford NER (CRF Classifier: 2012 Version) of Named Entity

NER Class	FrameNet	
	No. Frames	Frame Examples
PERSON	9	People (*e.g. person, lady, boy, man, woman*) People_by_vocation (*e.g. police_officer, journalist*)
ORGANIZATION	9	Bussiness (*e.g. company, corporation, firm*) Organization (*e.g. governent , agency, comittee*)
LOCATION	12	Locale (*e.g. earth, region, site, gzone, place*) Relational_natural_features (*e.g. lake, mountain*)
TIME	2	Calenderic_unit (*e.g. morning, evening, noon, eve*) Location _in _time (*e.g. time*)
DATE	2	Calenderic_unit (*e.g. winter, spring, summer*) Natural features (*e.g. spring, fall*)
MONEY	1	Money (*e.g. money, cash, funds*)
PERCENT	-	-

TABLE 3 – Information adopted from FrameNet

Recognizer (Finkel *et al.*, 2005) to label sequence of words indicating 7 types of entities (*PERSON, ORGANIZATION, LOCATION, TIME, DATE, MONEY* and *PERCENT*). The Stanford NER generally retrieves proper nouns from corresponding sentences and categorize into one of the mentioned class, as shown in the following example:

S1: *On Jan./DATE 5/DATE, a 15-year-old boy crashed a stolen plane into a building in Tampa/LOCATION, Florida/LOCATION.*

As Stanford NER only recognizes proper nouns, the common noun such as "*boy*" in the context is not labeled as *PERSON*. Thus, in order to harvest maximum information from a text span, we make use of the lexical units obtained from lexical database, FrameNet (Fillmore *et al.* 2003). We extracted lexical unit from FrameNet which matches the 7 class defined by Stanford NER class. The manual lexical unit extraction is carried out by 2 human judges. Table 3 shows the example of frames used in the experiment. We used data from FrameNet to retrieve the unidentified type of information from common noun in sentences. We hereafter refer to the information retrieved here and by Stanford NER as sentences entity. We computed the number of sentences entities appearing in both S_1 and S_2. Based on the study of training data from CSTBank, there are no significant examples of annotated sentences indicates which entity points to any particular discourse relation. Therefore, in the experiment, we only observed the number of sentences entities in both text spans. The features with higher number of entities are set to 1, and 0 for lower value.

2. Number of conjunctions

We observed the occurrence of 40 types of conjunctions. We measured the number of conjunctions appear in both S_1 and S_2. The feature with higher number of entities is set to 1, and 0 for lower value.

3. Lengths of sentences

We defined the length of S_j as follows:

$$Len(S_j) = \sum_{w_i \in S_j} w \qquad (8)$$

where w is the word appearing in the corresponding text span.

4. Type of Speech

We determined the type of speech, whether the text span, S_l cites another sentence by detecting the occurrence of quotation marks to identify *Citation* or *Indirect Speech* which are the sub-category of *Identity*.

3.3 Discourse Relations based Clustering Algorithm

Connections between two sentences can be represented by multiple discourse relations. For instance, in some cases, sentences defined as *Subsumption* can also be define as *Identity*. As we proposed a method of cluster generation of similar sentences, applying the same process against the same sentence pairs will be redundant. Therefore to reduce redundancy, we assigned the strongest relation to represent each connection according to the following order:

(i) whether both sentences are identical or not
(ii) whether one sentence includes another
(iii) whether both sentences share partial information
(iv) whether both sentences share the same subject of topic
(v) whether one sentence discusses any entity mentioned in another

The priority of the discourse relations assignment can be concluded as follows:

Identity > *Subsumption* > *Elaboration* > *Overlap* > *Change of Topics* > *Description*

We then performed clustering algorithm to construct groups of similar sentences. The algorithm is summarized as follows:

i) Assign the strongest relations determined by SVMs to each connection (refer to Figure 1(a)).

ii) Suppose each sentence is a centroid of its own cluster. Identify sentences connected to the centroid as *Identity (ID), Subsumption (SUB), Elaboration (ELA)* and *Overlap (OVE)* relations[1]. Sentences with these connections are evaluated as having similar content, and aggregated as one cluster (refer Figure 1(b)).

iii) Remove similar clusters by retrieving centroids connected as *Identity*, *Subsumption* or *Elaboration*.

iv) Merge the clusters from (iii) to minimize the occurrence of the same sentences in multiple clusters (refer Figure 1(c)).

v) Iterate step (iii) and (iv) until the number of clusters is convergence.

---

[1] We performed 2 types of text clustering, which includes and excludes *Overlap*

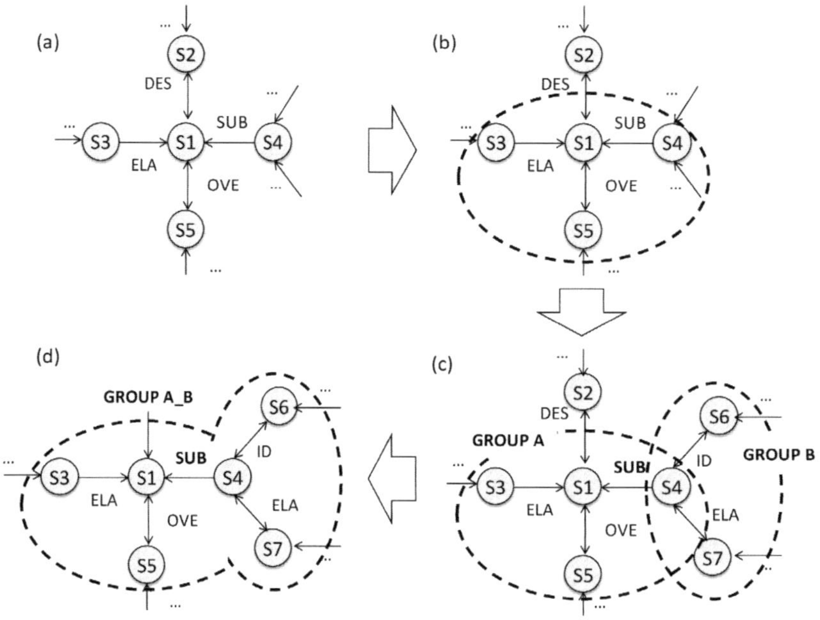

FIGURE 1 – Clustering algorithm based on discourse relations.

4 Experiment

4.1 Data

CST-annotated sentences pairs are obtained from publicly available data set from Cross-document Structure Theory Bank (Radev *et al.*, 2004) and were combined into relations according to Table 2. We used 218 sentence pairs of *Identity*, 317 pairs of *Subsumption*, 58 pairs of *Elaboration*, 157 pairs of *Overlap*, 348 pairs of *Change of Topics*, 70 pairs of *Description* and 120 pairs of *No Relations*. Our system is evaluated using 2 data sets from Document Understanding Conference, which are DUC'2001 and DUC'2002. DUC'2001 and DUC'2002 provided 30 and 59 document sets consisting 10,412 and 14,790 sentences, respectively. We used Brill's Tagger (Brill, 1992) to POS-tag the sentences, and extracted content words and lemmas of the words.

4.2 Result and Discussion

4.2.1 Discourse Relation Identification

The discourse relations assigned between sentences by SVMs is manually evaluated by 2 human judges. Since no human annotation is available for DUC data sets, 5 times of random sampling consisting 100 sentence pairs is performed against each document set (DUC'2001 and DUC'2002). The human judges performed manual annotation against sentence pairs, and assessed if SVMs assigned the correct discourse relation to each pair. The correct discourse relation refers to either one of the discourse relations assigned by human judges in case of multiple relations exist between the two sentences. We also assigned the most frequent relations

Relations	DUC'2001			DUC'2002		
	Precision	Recall	F-measure	Precision	Recall	F-measure
Baseline	0.112	0.946	0.197	0.144	0.855	0.241
Identity	0.983	1.000	0.991	0.855	1.000	0.921
Subsumption	0.688	0.985	0.804	0.685	0.900	0.773
Elaboration	0.650	0.952	0.768	0.644	0.902	0.737
Overlap	0.776	0.652	0.703	0.740	0.694	0.715
Change of Topics	0.553	0.701	0.614	0.611	0.593	0.597
Description	0.797	0.947	0.853	0.818	0.856	0.828
No Relations	0.969	0.556	0.697	0.985	0.652	0.782

TABLE 4 – Evaluation result for classification of discourse relations

to all sentence pairs as a baseline method. We used the precision, recall and F-measure score as an evaluation measure.

Table 4 shows the macro average of precision, recall and F-measure for DUC'2001 and DUC'2002**.** Evaluation results from Table 4 indicates that SVMs works well for the classification of *Identity*, *Subsumption*, *Elaboration* and *Overlap,* where the F-measure values achieved are above 70% for both data sets. In contrast, the F-measure value of *Change of Topics* shows an average result due to lack of significant characteristics which caused false positive result for sentence pairs with no relation. The following sentence pair shows the example of false positive result of *Change of Topics.*

S_{11} : *Boston have skyline, 2 1/2 miles in the distance, can seem so far away.*
S_{12} : *Though an interpreter, Martinez said he started out running 5:15 or 5:20 miles.*

The examples show that the *subject of the verb* in both sentences is different and both sentences semantically represent no relation with each other. Consider another example:

S_{13} : *The eight day trip will leave from Chicago and will include sightseeing, guided runs and fun run from Malahide Castle to Swords.*
S_{14} : *I had to have patience and run from the back.*

Both sentences were identified as *Overlap* by SVMs while there is no relation present between the sentences. As a result, the low recall value affected the F-measure of *No Relations*. Overall, classification by SVMs shows that our method outperformed over the baseline method, where our system achieved more than 60% accuracy for most relations even though we only consider surface characteristics from sentence pairs during classification.

4.2.2 Discourse Relation-based Clustering

We evaluated our method by measuring the cohesion and separation of the constructed clusters (Raskutti and Leckie, 1999) (IBM SPSS Statistics, 2011). The cluster cohesion refers to how closely the sentences are related within a cluster, measured using *Sum of Squared Errors (SSE)*;

$$AverageSSE = \frac{1}{N}\sum_{i}\sum_{x \in C_i} sim(x, m_i)^2 \qquad (9)$$

where *sim* (x,m_i) refers to the similarity of sentence x with other members in the same cluster, m_i and N denotes the number of clusters. The smaller value of *SSE* indicates that the sentences in clusters are closer to each other. Meanwhile, cluster separation refers to how distinct or well-separated a cluster from others, measured using *Sum of Squares Between* (*SSB*);

$$AverageSSB = \frac{1}{N}\sum_i |C_i| sim(m, m_i)^2 \tag{10}$$

where $sim(m,m_i)$ refers the similarity between sentences from the corresponding cluster with sentences outside the cluster, $|C_i|$ is the size of cluster and N is the number of clusters. The high value of *SSB* indicates that the sentences are well separated with each other. Cosine similarity measurement is used to measure the similarity between sentences in both *SSE* and *SSB* evaluation. We also obtained the average of *Silhouette Coefficient* (*SC*) to measure the harmonic mean of both cohesion and separation of the clusters (Kaufman and Rousseeuw, 1990) (IBM SPSS Statistics, 2011) by using Equation (11);

$$AverageSC = \frac{1}{N}(1 - \frac{a}{b}) \quad \text{if } a < b \text{ or,}$$

$$= \frac{1}{N}(\frac{b}{a} - 1) \quad \text{if } a \geq b \tag{11}$$

where a is the average similarity of sentence i with other members in the cluster, and b is the minimum average distance of sentence i with sentences outside the cluster and N is the number of clusters. The value range of the *Silhouette Coefficient* is between 0 and 1, where the value closer to 1 is the better.

Table 5 shows the evaluation results of text clustering. *Method1* refers to the clusters constructed by *Identity, Subsumption* and *Elaboration*, while *Method2* refers to the clusters constructed by *Identity, Subsumption, Elaboration* and *Overlap*. We also used *K-Means* clustering for comparison. *K-means* iteratively reassigns sentences to the closest clusters until a convergence criterion is met (McQueen, 1967). Evaluation results indicate that *Method1,* which generates clusters of sentences with strong connections (*Identity, Subsumption, and Elaboration*) demonstrates the best *SSE* value (4.181 for DUC'2001 and 3.624 for DUC'2002), which shows the most significant cohesion within clusters. In contrast, *Method2* which includes *Overlap* during clustering indicates the most significant separation between clusters with the best *SSB* value (397.237 for DUC'2001 and 257.118 for DUC'2002). *Method2* generated bigger clusters, therefore resulted wider separation from other clusters. Overall, the average of *Silhouette Coefficient* shows that our method, *Method1* (0.628 for DUC'2001 and 0.639 for DUC'2002) and *Method2* (0.652 for DUC'2001 and 0.636 for DUC'2002) outranked *K-Means* (0.512 for DUC'2001 and 0.510 for DUC'2002) for both data sets.

In addition, we examined the clustered sentences by using a pair-wise evaluation measure, where we sampled 5 sets of data consisting 100 sentences pairs and evaluated if both sentences are actually belong to the same clusters. Table 6 shows the macro average Precision, Recall and F-measure for pair-wise evaluation. *Method1*, which excludes *Overlap* relation during clustering, demonstrated a lower Recall value compared to *Method2* and *K-Means*. However, the Precision score of *Method1* indicates better performance compared to *K-Means*. Overall, *Method2* obtained the best value for all measurement compared to *Method1* and *K-Means* for both data sets. We achieved optimum pair-wise results by including *Overlap* during clustering, where the F-measure

Clustering Method	DUC'2001			DUC'2002		
	Average SSE	Average SSB	Average SC	Average SSE	Average BSS	Average SC
K-Means	7.271	209.111	0.512	6.991	154.511	0.510
Method1 (ID, SUB, ELA)	4.181	308.153	0.628	3.624	214.762	0.639
Method2 (ID, SUB, ELA,OVE)	4.599	397.237	0.652	3.927	257.118	0.636

TABLE 5 –Evaluation result for cohesion and separation of the clusters

Clustering Method	DUC'2001			DUC'2002		
	Precision	Recall	F-measure	Precision	Recall	F-measure
K-Means	0.577	0.898	0.702	0.603	0.885	0.716
Method1 (ID, SUB, ELA)	0.805	0.590	0.678	0.750	0.533	0.623
Method2 (ID, SUB, ELA,OVE)	0.783	0.758	0.770	0.779	0.752	0.766

TABLE 6 – Evaluation result for pair-wise

obtained for DUC'2001 and DUC'2002 are 0.770 and 0.766, respectively.

We can see from Table 5 and Table 6 that the connection between sentences can allow text clustering according to the user preference. For instance, sentences with *Identity*, *Subsumption* and *Elaboration* were classified into a small group without overlapping with other clusters. In contrast, sentences with *Identity*, *Subsumption*, *Elaboration* and *Overlap* allow minimum information overlapping between clusters. Thus, the experimental results demonstrate that the utilization of discourse relation can be another alternative of cluster construction other than observing word distribution in corpus.

Conclusion and perspectives

This paper explored the benefits of discourse relation in data mining. The evaluation results showed that the discourse relation-based method has promising potential as a novel approach for text clustering. Our method is capable to offer various kind of text clustering, such as clustering of only identical or overlapping sentences. In future, addition of other types of relations, *e.g.*, *Attribution* (from CST) can be used to perform clustering of attributed information from corpus. Previously, discourse relation has been used to remove redundancy from generated summaries, thus, sentence clustering based on discourse relations will definitely benefits text summarization for multiple documents. Our future works will include (i) the investigation of more discourse relations for text clustering, (ii) to improve the classification of discourse relations, and (iii) the application of discourse relation-based clustering to text summarization.

References

Mann, W.C. and Thompson, S.A., "Discourse Structure Theory: A Theory of Text Organization", Technical Report ISI/RS-87-190, ISI, Los Angeles, California, 1987.

Carlson, L., Marcu, D. and Okurowski, M.E., "RST Discourse Treebank", Linguistic Data Consortium 1-58563-223-6, 2002.

Webber, B.L., Knott, A., Stone, M. and Joshi, A., "Anaphora and Discourse Structure", Computational Linguistics 29 (4), pp. 545–588, 2003.

Radev, D.R., Ottherbacher, J. and Zhang, Z., "CSTBank: A Corpus for the Study of Cross-document Structural Relationship", In Proc. of Language Resource and Evaluation Conference (LREC), 2004.

Wolf, F., Gibson, E., Fisher, A. and Knight, M.,"Discourse Graphbank", Linguistic Data Consortium, Philadelphia, 2005.

Vapnik, V., "The Nature of Statistical Learning Theory", Springer, New York, 1995.

Marcu, D., "From Discourse Structures to Text Summaries", In Proc. of the Association for Computational Linguistics (ACL) on Intelligent Scalable Text Summarization, pp. 82-88, 1997.

Radev, D.R., Jing, H., Sty,M., and Tam, D.,"Centroid-based Summarization of Multiple Documents", Inf. Process.Manage.(40), pp. 919-938, 2004.

Zhang, Z., Blair-Goldensohn, S. and Radev, D.R., "Towards CST-enhanced Summarization", In Proc. of the 18th National Conference on Artificial Intelligence (AAAI) , 2002.

Uzêda, V.R., Pardo, T.A.S., Nunes, M.G.V.,"A Comprehensive Summary Informativeness Evaluation for RST-based Summarization Methods", International Journal of Computer Information Systems and Industrial Management Applications (IJCISIM) ISSN: 2150-7988 Vol.1, pp.188-196, 2009.

Louis, A., Joshi, A., and Nenkova, A., "Discourse Indicators for Content Selection in Summarization", In Proc. of 11th Annual Meeting of the Special Interest Group on Discourse and Dialogue (SIGDIAL), pp. 147-156, 2010.

Litkowski, K., "CL Research Experiments in TREC-10 Question Answering", The 10th Text Retrieval Conference (TREC 2001). NIST Special Publication, pp. 200-250, 2002.

Verberne, S., Boves, L., and Oostdijk, N., "Discourse-based Answering of *Why*-Questions", Traitement Automatique des Langues, special issue on Computational Approaches to Discourse and Document Processing, pp. 21-41, 2007.

Theune, M., "Contrast in Concept-to-speech Generation", Computer Speech & Language,16(3-4), ISSN 0885-2308, pp. 491-530, 2002.

Piwek, P. and Stoyanchev, S., " Generating Expository Dialogue from Monologue Motivation, Corpus and Preliminary Rules", In Proc. of 11th Annual Conference of the North American Chapter of the Association for Computational Linguistics (NAACL), 2010.

Jorge, M.L.C and Pardo, T.S., "Experiments with CST-based Multi-document Summarization", Workshop on Graph-based Methods for Natural Language Processing, Association for Computational Linguistics (ACL), pp. 74-82, 2010.

Lin, D., "PRINCIPAR- An Efficient, Broad-coverage, Principle-based Parser", In Proc. of 15th International Conference on Computational Linguistics (COLING), pg.482-488, 1994.

Finkel, J.R., Grenager, T. and Manning, C., "Incorporating Non-local Information into Information Extraction Systems by Gibbs Sampling", In Proc. of the 43rd Annual Meeting of the Association for Computational Linguistics (ACL), pp. 363-370, 2005.

Fillmore, C.J., Baker, C.F., and Lowe, J.,B., "FrameNet and Software Tools", In Proc. of 17th International Conference on Computational Linguistics (COLING), 36th Annual Meeting of the Association for Computational Linguistics (ACL), pp. 86-90,1998.

Radev, D.R., Otterbacher, J. and Zhang, Z., "CSTBank: Cross-document Structure Theory Bank", http://tangra.si.umich.edu/clair/CSTBank/phase1.htm

Brill, E., "A Simple Rule-based Part-of-Speech Tagger", In Proc. of 3rd Conference on Applied Natural Language Processing, pp. 152-155, 1992.

Raskutti, B. and C. Leckie, "An Evaluation of Criteria for Measuring the Quality of Clusters", In Proc. of the 16th International Joint Conference on Artificial Intelligence, ISBN:1-55860-613-0, pp: 905-910,1999.

IBM SPSS Statistic Database, "Cluster Evaluation Algorithm" http://publib.boulder.ibm.com/ , 2011

Kaufman, L. and Rousseeuw, P., "Finding Groups in Data: An Introduction to Cluster Analysis", John Wiley and Sons, London. ISBN: 10: 0471878766, 1990.

McQueen, J., "Some Methods for Classification and Analysis of Multivariate Observations", In Proc. of the 5th Berkeley Symposium on Mathematical Statistics and Probability, pp. 281–297, 1967.

Measuring the Strength of Linguistic Cues for Discourse Relations

Fatemeh Torabi Asr and Vera Demberg
Cluster of Excellence Multimodal Computing and Interaction (MMCI)
Saarland University
Campus C7.4, 66123 Saarbrücken, Germany
fatemeh@coli.uni-saarland.de, vera@coli.uni-saarland.de

Abstract

Discourse relations in the recent literature are typically classified as either explicit (e.g., when a discourse connective like "because" is present) or implicit. This binary treatment of implicitness is advantageous for simplifying the explanation of many phenomena in discourse processing. On the other hand, linguists do not yet agree as to what types of textual particles contribute to revealing the relation between any pair of sentences or clauses in a text. At one extreme, we can claim that every single word in either of the sentences involved can play a role in shaping a discourse relation. In this work, we propose a measure to quantify how good a cue a certain textual element is for a specific discourse relation, i.e., a measure of the *strength* of discourse markers. We will illustrate how this measure becomes important both for modeling discourse relation construction as well as developing automatic tools for identifying discourse relations.

Keywords: Discourse relations, Discourse markers, Discourse cues, Implicitness, Implicit and explicit relations.

Proceedings of the Workshop on Advances in Discourse Analysis and its Computational Aspects (ADACA), pages 33–42,
COLING 2012, Mumbai, December 2012.

1 Introduction

Clauses, sentences and larger segments of a text should be connected to one another for a text to be coherent. A connection in the semantic-pragmatic level is established with the help of sharing entities in the discourse or relations between statements, which are called *discourse relations*. The discourse relations are usually described in terms of their relation sense (e.g., causal, temporal, additive). Identification of these relations, i.e., first coming up with a set of possible relation senses and then assigning labels to the segments of a given text, is an essential first step in both theoretical and application-based studies on discourse processing. Given a set of sense labels (like the ones in the Penn Discourse Treebank (PDTB, Prasad et al., 2008)), identification of the relations between neighboring segments of a text is a difficult task when the text segments do not include an explicit discourse connector. For example, in (1-a) the connective "because" is a marker of a causal relation between the two clauses, whereas in (1-b) the relation is not marked explicitly with a discourse connector.

(1) a. Bill took his daughter to the hospital, because she looked pale and sick in the morning.
    b. I was very tired last night. I went to sleep earlier than usual.

The presence of explicit cues makes it easier for humans to infer discourse relations during comprehension of a text or an utterance. Similarly, explicit discourse connectors have been shown to help the automatic identification of these relations for NLP tools (Pitler et al., 2008). In fact, choosing a set of relation types in preparing discourse-level annotated corpora is often done with reference to the well-known lexical or phrasal discourse markers[1]. A good example is the procedure used by the annotators of the Penn Discourse Treebank (PDTB) to identify implicit relations in the corpus[2]. Some relations are associated with discourse cues which mark them almost unambiguously (e.g., "because" for a causal relation), while other discourse relations typically occur with no explicit marker (e.g., list relations), or tend to be expressed using markers which are ambiguous (e.g., synchronous temporal relations are usually marked by "while", which can also be a cue for juxtaposition). One can look at this ambiguity from a different perspective: some discourse markers such as "but" are used in almost every type of adversative context, whereas a marker such as "unless" is used only for a very specific type of relation (disjunctive).

In this paper, we try to elaborate on the two-way link between discourse markers and the relation senses that are typically used in the literature. We propose a quantification of the cue *strength*, i.e., how well a discourse marker makes a discourse relation explicit in the text. Based on the numbers we extract from the PDTB, we suggest that implicitness should be treated as a continuum and not as a binary feature of a discourse relation. The rest of this paper is organized as follows: Section 2 introduces the probabilistic measure we use to estimate the strength of a discourse cue in marking a particular discourse relation between segments of a text. Section 3 includes a brief introduction of the PDTB hierarchy of relation senses, statistics about distribution of implicit and explicit relations, and specifically, the

[1] We use the terms *discourse marker* and *discourse cue* interchangeably in this paper. Nevertheless, *cue* is used more typically when the predictive nature of the textual element is highlighted (see Müller (2005) for a discussion on the terminology).

[2] As the case study reported in this paper has been done on the PDTB, we adapt their terminology when referring to different types of discourse cues and senses of discourse relations.

strength measurements we performed on the annotated discourse connectives in the corpus. In the last section we discuss why and how consideration of the cue strength would help theoretical and application-based studies of discourse processing.

2 Quantification of the Marking Strength

A discourse relation is established between two (or more) segments of a text each of which includes several words or phrases. Applying a formal logic approach (like the one by Sanders et al. (1992)) would suggest that discourse relation establishment is an operation which takes place between independent arguments (statements) by means of explicit operators (discourse cues) or the relational semantics we obtain implicitly from the text according to our world knowledge. Although all words in the arguments contribute to the shaping of the relation, discourse cues as defined in the literature typically refer to a specific category of words or phrases which have an operator-like function in the discourse level. For example, Stede (2011) distinguishes discourse *connectives* as closed-class, non-inflectable words or word groups syntactically from adverbial, subordinate/coordinate conjunction, or preposition categories which themselves can only be interpreted successfully when they appear in a relation between two discourse segments. (Prasad et al., 2010), however, suggest that a variety of expressions exist that mark discourse relations, but they are not from the typically-considered syntactic categories, and in some places they are not even structurally frozen (e.g., "that would follow").

Whatever syntactic or sematic function a discourse cue is associated with, the relative frequency of its occurrence in a particular type of discourse relation is what makes it interesting. Our focus is not on the structural properties of a discourse marker, but instead on the strength of the marker for indicating a specific discourse relation. Given a segment of a text, perhaps composed of two sentences whose discourse relation is to be determined, one would think about a set of cues that express the polarity and temporality of the sentences, the stated relation between the involved entities, as well as the presence of any word or expression that can be attributed to a specific discourse relation. A simple probabilistic model would look for a relation r which maximizes $p(r|cues)$. For estimating the probability of a discourse relation r given a cue cue, we can use Bayes' theorem to formulate:

$$p(r|cue) = \frac{p(cue|r)}{p(cue)} * p(r) \tag{1}$$

where $p(r)$ is the prior probability of relation r, and $\frac{p(cue|r)}{p(cue)}$ determines the effect of the present discourse cue in identification of r, namely, the *strength* of the cue. If a word or expression is a good marker for a particular relation, we would expect it to have a high strength value. It would mean that the cue is seen in many instances of that relation relative to its total number of occurrences. We propose that the strength of a discourse marker is a reliable measure one can use to estimate how well that cue would work in a discourse relation identification task, be it by human comprehenders, annotators or computational automated tools.

3 Case study: PDTB

The Penn Discourse Treebank (Prasad et al., 2008) includes annotations of 18,459 explicit and 16,053 implicit discourse relations in texts from the Wall Street Jounal. Explicit

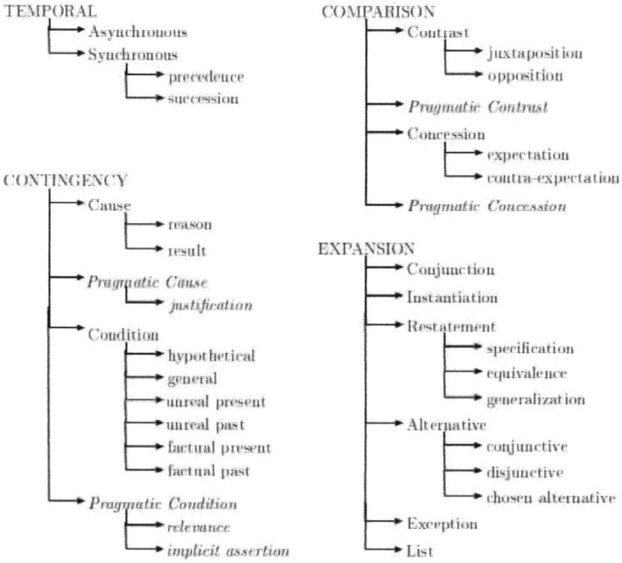

Figure 1: Hierarchy of senses in PDTB (Prasad et al., 2008)

relations are those expressed through one out of a closed-class set of discourse connective in the original text. After the annotation of explicit discourse connectors, annotators were asked to decide on the discourse relationship between any two adjacent sentences in the corpus which were not already linked through explicit connectors, and insert one or more suitable discourse connectives. Labeling of the relations is done according to a hierarchy of senses (see Figure 1), including four top-level classes: `CONTINGENCY`, `COMPARISON`, `TEMPORAL` and `EXPANSION`. In most of the cases the relation sense is chosen from the deepest possible level of the hierarchy (leaves of the tree). But when the annotators did not agree on the fine-grained relation sense (e.g., `Instantiation`), they compromised by tagging the relation with a more general sense (`EXPANSION` in this case).

In our study of cue strength, we decided to analyze only those relations for which the most specific tagging was available, i.e., those tagged with one of the 30 relation senses in the leaves of the hierarchy. In this set of relations we found 95 connective types which appeared in the explicit relations and 70 connective types used for annotation of the implicit relations. Strength values reported in this paper are calculated according to the explicit occurrences of a particular connective for a particular relation sense in the mentioned subset of text extracted from the PDTB. The strength values range between 0.0028 and 71.4370 after applying simple add-1 smoothing to avoid division by zero[3].

3.1 Implicit vs. Explicit Relations

First of all, by looking at the overall distribution of relation types, we found a significant difference between implicit and explicit occurrences. Some types of relations tend to appear implicitly (e.g., `List`, `Instantiation`, and `Restatement`) while some others almost always appear with their markers (e.g., subtypes of `Condition`). Distributions of discourse cues

[3]We made a 2-d matrix with connective type vs. relation type dimensions and added 1 to the frequency appearing in each cell. Then we calculated $\frac{p(cue|r)}{p(cue)}$ according to the resulting frequency table.

also differ to a similar extent between implicit and explicit occurrences, as relation senses and the discourse cues are highly correlated.

A smaller set of connectives appears to have been employed by annotators for the implicit relations. There are two possible reasons for this: first, some connectives such as "if" are markers of relations which cannot easily be expressed without a discourse connective. (For example, "if" is only used for explicit conditionals, and conditional discourse relations are expressed almost always with an explicit connector, so that no implicit "if" was annotated). A second possible reason for a connective not to appear frequently in the implicit annotations is if there exists a connective which is a better cue, or is much more frequent and has a similar function. An interesting case is the connective "when" which appears only a few times implicitly. One type of relation that this connective marks is the `reason` relation, which is very frequent in both implicit and explicit instances. The strongest marker of the `reason` relation is the connective "because" (11.80 strength), which makes it a better candidate when annotating implicit `reason` relations, compared to "when" (1.13 strength).

3.2 The Most Reliable Cues

The first thing we wanted to investigate by looking at the table of strength measurements was to find out which of the 95 connective types under study could most reliably mark a particular relation sense. To do this, we first looked at the strength measurements for frequent connectives. Among the 20 most frequent connectives in the corpus, a few showed a high strength score: "for example" for the `Instantiation` relation (42.17), "although" and "though" for the `expectation` relation (23.34 and 18.44), and "so" for the `result` relation (20.36). The highly frequent connectives "and" and "but" are associated with relatively small specificity scores (distributed strength) over a number of relation senses.

We found that 45 out of 95 connective types are used most frequently in some relation which is not the most specific relation they mark. Table 1 shows the strength scores and frequencies of six such connectives. It suggests that a number of relation instances including these connectives are not strongly marked. For example, "while" is used in many places as the connective of a `Synchrony` relation, but the negative bias in its meaning makes it a more reliable cue for an `opposition` relation, and the `Synchrony` relation is most reliably marked with "when" and "as". Nevertheless, there is a subset of fairly frequent connectives which are associated with a very high strength to mark specific relation types. It includes

Connective	Most frequent relation	Strongest marking
and	Conjunction (2724, 3.04)	List (211, 3.71)
but	Juxtaposition (640, 6.54)	Contra-expectation (497, 7.20)
however	Juxtaposition (90, 6.01)	Contra-expectation (71, 6.72)
indeed	Conjunction (55, 1.57)	Specification (33, 24.39)
nor	Conjunction (27, 1.61)	Conjunctive (5, 11.15)
while	Synchrony (242, 3.72)	Opposition (91, 5.16)

Table 1: Comparison between the most frequent relation that a connective marks and the relation it marks with the highest strength (numbers in the brackets are the frequency of use and the strength of the connective for that relation, respectively).

"instead" for the `chosen alternative` (71.44), "or" for `conjunctive` (63.31) and "unless" for disjunctive (61.96). These connectives can be distinguished as very strong discourse markers with respect to the PDTB hierarchy of senses.

3.3 The Strongly Marked Relations

In the next step, we looked at different relation types to see which are most reliably marked by the connectives. We found that 12 out of 30 relation senses are most frequently marked with some connective that was not the most specific marker of that relation. Table 2 shows statistics for a number of such relations. In some cases, the strength associated with the typical marker is not very different from the maximum strength value obtained over all connectives for that relation. For example, `Conjunction` relations are usually marked by "and", which exhibits a fairly similar strength score to "also", i.e., the strongest marker of the relation. Although usage of "also" is very specific to the `Conjunction` relation, the small $p(cue|r)$ results in a relatively weak link between the relation and the connective. For some relations there is a big difference between the strength of the most frequently used connective and that of the strongest connective. A good example is `contra-expectation`, which in most cases appears in the corpus with "but", a very generally used connective with a distributed marking strength over a variety of relation types. This would suggest that this relation type is usually not very strongly marked (as it could be marked by the use of "still" for example). We also investigated the variance of the strength values obtained over connective types for a particular relation. Interestingly, we found that the smallest variance of strength values was again obtained by the `Conjunction` relation, the most frequent relation in the corpus for which a number of connectives are used. We could imagine that if the `Conjunction` relation was divided into two or several subtypes (one might get help from the instances in which "also" is used to see whether a more specific relation sense can be considered), then each of those subtypes would be associated to a significantly greater strength of their cues.

Relation	Most frequent connective		Strongest marker	
Contra-expectation	but	(497, 7.20)	still	(81, 12.22)
Opposition	but	(177, 5.04)	on the other hand	(10, 8.16)
Factual present	if	(77, 6.18)	if then	(10, 14.86)
Pragmatic concession	but	(9, 1.06)	nevertheless	(6, 16.80)
Pragmatic contrast	but	(31, 3.18)	insofar as	(1, 4.93)
Conjunction	and	(2724, 3.04)	also	(1736, 3.50)
List	and	(211, 3.71)	finally	(8, 6.94)
Synchrony	when	(595, 5.64)	as	(544, 6.59)

Table 2: Comparison between the most frequent connective that marks a relation and the strongest marker of it (numbers in the brackets are the frequency of use and the strength of the connective for that relation, respectively).

4 Discussion and Conclusions

We reported examples of our measurements of discourse connective strength in reflecting relational senses. In this section, we will discuss how looking at the strength of discourse markers could be helpful in studies about discourse relations.

4.1 Development of the Corpora

Recent research on discourse processing, like other linguistic studies, is paying considerable attention to the corpus analysis. For this, a number of multi-purpose corpora of discourse-level annotated data, such as PDTB (Prasad et al., 2008) and RST-DTB (Carlson et al., 2003), have been developed. There are many theoretical and technical issues that need to be considered in developing such databases, some of which we think are relevant to our study of discourse markers:

Relation senses are not easy to define, especially when a corpus is being developed for a variety of research interests. Since discourse markers are the most important features one can use for defining (or choosing among previously-defined) discourse relation senses, statistics such as the strength of the cue become important. For example, the strength values of discourse cues marking the `Conjunction` relation are rather low. A different or more fine-grained division into subtypes for this relation might be worth considering.

Cross-corpora checking of the taxonomies (used for labeling discourse relations) could be useful in order to refine relation sense hierarchies. Van Dijk (2004) suggests that a discourse relation could either be of a *functional* type to establish intentional coherence between propositions in a text (e.g., the one proposition is a generalization / explanation / specification of the other), or of a referential type which expresses some extensional coherence between facts underlying the sentences (e.g., the facts stand in some causal / conditional / temporal relationship). He adds that these two types of relations have been confused in the literature (e.g., in RST Corpora) and need to be distinguished from one another. We believe that marker strength is potentially good means of studying the fine-grained classification of discourse relations, to distinguish for example between intensional and extensional coherence. Comparison of the relations tagged in two corpora with respect to the cue strength measurements might be helpful to find the overlaps or variance between relation sense definitions.

Implicit vs. explicit annotations of discourse relations are so far done simply according to the presence of *any* discourse connective. We would expect that in the near future many theoretical studies about discourse comprehension will be carried out on the basis of the available annotations. In such studies, the implicitness of a particular relation in a text should not be investigated solely in terms of the presence of a discourse marker. The markedness would strongly rely on the strength of the link between the relation type and the applied discourse cue and should be treated as a continuous feature. For example, `Reason` relations in the corpus which include "and" as their connective, are not really explicit causal relations, rather the causality is left implicit in the content of the arguments (this could further inform recent studies such as the one by Asr and Demberg (2012)).

4.2 Automatic Identification of Discourse Relations

Another aspect which is particularly important for computational linguists and NLP researchers is to develop a methods for automatically identifying discourse relations in a given text or utterance – which happens after defining a set of desired relation senses. We would suggest consideration of the following points both for human annotators and for development of automatic tools:

Discourse cues should be looked at with respect to their specificity, e.g., the measure we proposed to determine the marking strength of a word group. Every phrase or word in a discourse relation could be counted as a cue, especially, when typically closed-class discourse connectives are not present. One example class of such markers are implicit causality verbs whose presence in a sentence can mark an upcoming reason (Asr and Demberg, 2012; Rohde and Horton, 2010). Another example is the presence of negation and / or downward-entailing verbs as a cue for an upcoming `chosen alternative` relation (Webber, 2012). Further examples include AltLex (Prasad et al., 2010), namely, alternative lexicaliztation of specific relations (e.g., "the reason is that...") which might even be stronger markers than many of conjunctions such as "and" or "but". The strength measure we proposed in this paper can be applied to any of these classes of cues, regardless of the syntactic differences. Only a strong cue can trigger expectation for a semantic/pragmatic relation between statements, thus, coherence of a text. On the other hand, mere presence of a sentence connective is a matter of textual cohesion (Halliday and Hasan, 1976).

Features for identification of relations can range from blind and coarse-grain properties of the propositional arguments (e.g, temporal focus of the events) to very fine-grained properties of the included discourse cues. We showed that the strength of the cue is a meaningful term in a simple probabilistic modeling of relation identification. Strength values can be calculated directly from the distribution of the discourse cues in a given corpus. Indeed, such a term should be used in a clear formulation along with the prior probability of the relation, i.e., the general expectation for a particular relation. Researchers have examined the classification of explicit and implicit discourse relations by only looking at the most typical relation that a discourse connective marks and obtained good accuracy for a coarse classification(Pitler et al., 2008; Zhou et al., 2010). To get an acceptable result for identification of fine-grained relation senses, one should definitely look into the strength of the discourse cue as some of them might not be reliable markers in a given context. Furthermore, it has been found that implicit relations are very difficult to classify correctly when learning only on explicit discourse relations (Sporleder, 2008). We would expect that weakly marked relations are similar to the unmarked relations; hence, one could possibly make use of this subset of explicit relations as training data for identification of implicit relations and get a different result.

4.3 Conclusions

This paper suggests a measure for the strength of a discourse cue in terms of its association with a specific discourse relation. We calculate this cue strength for discourse connectors and discourse relations as annotated in the Penn Discourse Treebank. We propose that such measurements are needed to understand how explicitly a discourse relation is marked in a text and what types of relations can be identified reliably by the use of their specific markers. Our findings also encourage the usage of a measure of cue strength in order to refine and develop robust annotations of discourse relation senses. We believe that theoretical as well as application-based studies in the field should in one way or another look into the strength of the link between the specific usage of words and phrases in a text and the type of coherence relation they reflect. Our preliminary findings can count as a trigger for future studies on discourse relations, the formalism and automated methods to identify them with respect to different types of discourse markers.

References

Asr, F. T. and Demberg, V. (2012). Implicitness of discourse relations. In *Proceedings of COLING*, Mumbai, India.

Carlson, L., Marcu, D., and Okurowski, M. (2003). Building a discourse-tagged corpus in the framework of rhetorical structure theory. *Current and new directions in discourse and dialogue*, pages 85–112.

Halliday, M. and Hasan, R. (1976). *Cohesion in English.* Longman (London).

Müller, S. (2005). Discourse markers in native and non-native english discourse. *Pragmatics and Beyond*, 138:1–297.

Pitler, E., Raghupathy, M., Mehta, H., Nenkova, A., Lee, A., and Joshi, A. (2008). Easily identifiable discourse relations. *Technical Reports (CIS)*, page 884.

Prasad, R., Dinesh, N., Lee, A., Miltsakaki, E., Robaldo, L., Joshi, A., and Webber, B. (2008). The Penn Discourse Treebank 2.0. In *Proceedings of the 6th International Conference on Language Resources and Evaluation*, pages 2961–2968.

Prasad, R., Joshi, A., and Webber, B. (2010). Realization of discourse relations by other means: alternative lexicalizations. In *Proceedings of the 23rd International Conference on Computational Linguistics: Posters*, pages 1023–1031.

Rohde, H. and Horton, W. (2010). Why or what next? eye movements reveal expectations about discourse direction. In *Proceedings of 23rd Annual CUNY Conference on Human Sentence Processing*, pages 18–20.

Sanders, T., Spooren, W., and Noordman, L. (1992). Toward a taxonomy of coherence relations. *Discourse Processes*, 15(1):1–35.

Sporleder, C. (2008). Lexical models to identify unmarked discourse relations: Does WordNet help? *Lexical-Semantic Resources in Automated Discourse Analysis*, page 20.

Stede, M. (2011). Discourse processing. *Synthesis Lectures on Human Language Technologies*, 4(3):1–165.

Van Dijk, T. (2004). From text grammar to critical discourse analysis. *A brief academic autobiography. version*, 2.

Webber, B. (2012). Alternatives and extra-propositional meaning. PASCAL 2 Invited Talk at ExProM Workshop, Jeju Island, Korea.

Zhou, Z., Xu, Y., Niu, Z., Lan, M., Su, J., and Tan, C. (2010). Predicting discourse connectives for implicit discourse relation recognition. In *Proceedings of the 23rd International Conference on Computational Linguistics: Posters*, pages 1507–1514.

Semi-Automatic Annotation of Intra-Sentential Discourse Relations in PDT

Pavlína Jínová, Jiří Mírovský and Lucie Poláková
Charles University in Prague
Institute of Formal and Applied Linguistics

{jinova|mirovsky|polakova}@ufal.mff.cuni.cz

ABSTRACT

In the present paper, we describe in detail and evaluate the process of semi-automatic annotation of intra-sentential discourse relations in the Prague Dependency Treebank, which is a part of the project of otherwise mostly manual annotation of all (intra- and inter-sentential) discourse relations with explicit connectives in the treebank. Our assumption that some syntactic features of a sentence analysis (in a form of a deep-syntax dependency tree) correspond to certain discourse-level features proved to be correct, and the rich annotation of the treebank allowed us to automatically detect the intra-sentential discourse relations, their connectives and arguments in most of the cases.

TITLE AND ABSTRACT IN CZECH

Poloautomatická anotace vnitrovětných diskurzních vztahů v PDT

ABSTRAKT

V tomto článku nabízíme detailní popis a evaluaci procesu poloautomatické anotace vnitrovětných textových vztahů v Pražském závislostním korpusu jako součást projektu jinak především manuální anotace všech (vnitro- a mezivětných) textových vztahů s explicitním konektorem v tomto korpusu. Potvrdil se náš předpoklad, že některé syntaktické vlastnosti analýzy věty (ve formě závislostního stromu hloubkové syntaxe) odpovídají jistým vlastnostem na úrovni analýzy textových vztahů (diskurzu). Bohatá anotace korpusu nám ve většině případů umožnila automaticky detekovat vnitrovětné vztahy, jejich konektory a argumenty.

KEYWORDS : TECTOGRAMMATICS, PDT, DISCOURSE ANNOTATION, INTRA-SENTENTIAL RELATIONS

KEYWORDS IN CZECH : TEKTOGRAMATIKA, PDT, ANOTACE DISKURZU, VNITROVĚTNÉ VZTAHY

Proceedings of the Workshop on Advances in Discourse Analysis and its Computational Aspects (ADACA), pages 43–58,
COLING 2012, Mumbai, December 2012.

1 Introduction

Linguistic phenomena going beyond the sentence boundary have been coming into the focus of computational linguists in the last decade. Various corpora annotated with discourse relations appear, two of the first and most influential (for English) were the RST Discourse Treebank (Carlson, Marcu, Okurowski, 2002) and Penn Discourse Treebank (Prasad et al., 2008). For other languages we can mention discourse-annotated resources for Turkish (Zeyrek et al., 2010), Arabic (Al-Saif and Markert, 2010), and Chinese (Zhou and Xue, 2012). Most of these projects have raw texts as their annotation basis. In the discourse project for Czech, contrary to the others, discourse-related phenomena have been annotated directly on top of the syntactic (tectogrammatical) trees of the Prague Dependency Treebank 2.5 (henceforth PDT, Bejček et al., 2012), with the goal to make maximum use of the syntactico-semantic information from the sentence representation.

The annotation of discourse relations (semantic relations between discourse units) in PDT consisted of two steps – first, the inter-sentential discourse relations were annotated manually, second, the intra-sentential discourse relations were annotated semi-automatically. In both cases, only relations signalled by an explicit discourse connective have been annotated.

The main goal of this paper is to report in detail on the process of the semi-automatic annotation of intra-sentential discourse relations in PDT. As we assumed, some of the (not only) syntactic features already annotated in the treebank were very helpful and enabled us to perform automatic extractions and conversions.[1] Nevertheless, some manual work had to be done both before and after the annotation.

1.1 Layers of Annotation in PDT

The data in our project come from the Prague Dependency Treebank 2.5 (Bejček et al., 2012), which is a corrected and enhanced version of PDT 2.0 (Hajič et al., 2006). PDT is a treebank of Czech written journalistic texts (almost 50 thousand sentences) enriched with a complex manual annotation at three layers: the morphological layer, where each token is assigned a lemma and a POS tag, the so-called analytical layer, at which the surface-syntactic structure of the sentence is represented as a dependency tree, and the tectogrammatical layer, at which the linguistic meaning of the sentence is represented.

At the tectogrammatical layer, the meaning of the sentence is represented as a dependency tree structure. Nodes of the tectogrammatical tree represent auto-semantic words, whereas functional words (such as prepositions, auxiliaries, subordinating conjunctions) and punctuation marks have (in most cases) no node of their own. The nodes are labelled with a large set of attributes, mainly with a tectogrammatical lemma and a functor (semantic relation; e.g. Predicate (PRED), Actor (ACT), Patient (PAT),

[1] For details on the exploitation of the syntactic features during the manual annotation of the inter-sentential relations, please consult Mírovský et al. (2012).

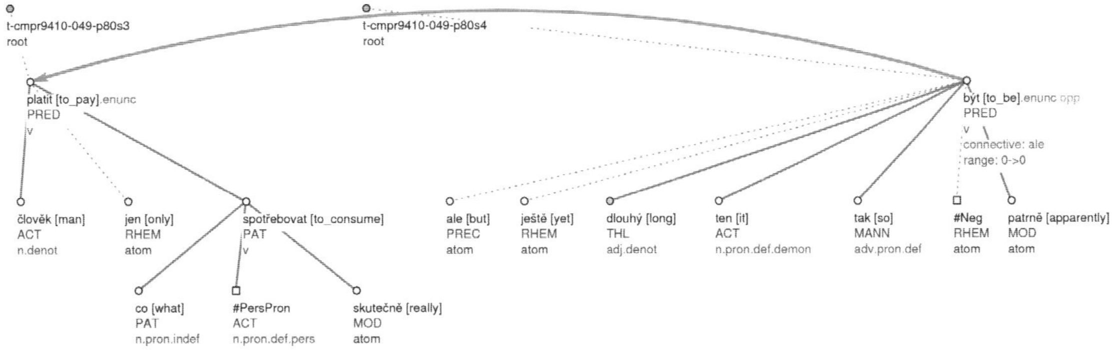

FIGURE 1 – An example of an inter-sentential discourse relation, represented by a thick arrow between roots of the arguments

Location (LOC))[2]. Additionally, the tectogrammatical layer includes the annotation of information structure attributes (sentence topic and focus, rhematizing expressions etc.).

1.2 Discourse Annotation in Two Steps

In the project of discourse annotation, we have focused on discourse relations anchored by an explicit (surface-present) discourse connective. These relations and their connectives have been annotated throughout the whole PDT. However, all the numbers reported in the paper refer to the training and development test parts of the whole data[3], i.e. 43,955 sentences (approx. 9/10 of the treebank).[4]

The annotation of discourse relations proceeded in two steps: First, the inter-sentential and some selected intra-sentential discourse relations were annotated manually, second, the remaining intra-sentential discourse relations were annotated (semi-)automatically, based on the information already annotated in PDT.[5]

The main theoretical principle of the annotation was the same for both phases. It was inspired partially by the lexical approach of the Penn Discourse Treebank project (Prasad et al., 2008), and partially by the tectogrammatical approach and the functional generative description (Sgall et al., 1986, Mikulová et al., 2005). A discourse connective in this view takes two text spans (verbal clauses or larger units) as its arguments. The semantic relation between the arguments is represented by a discourse arrow (link), the direction of which also uniformly defines the nature of the argument (e.g. reason – result).[6]

[2] For a description of functors in PDT, see http://ufal.mff.cuni.cz/pdt2.0/doc/manuals/en/t-layer/html/ch07.html.
[3] as distinguished in the PDT project
[4] Thus the last tenth of the treebank, evaluation test data, remains (as far as possible) unobserved.
[5] The annotation had to proceed in this order. Our understanding what is possible to annotate automatically only formed during the manual annotation, as we got familiar with the data.
[6] For further information on the annotation guidelines, see http://ufal.mff.cuni.cz/discourse/.

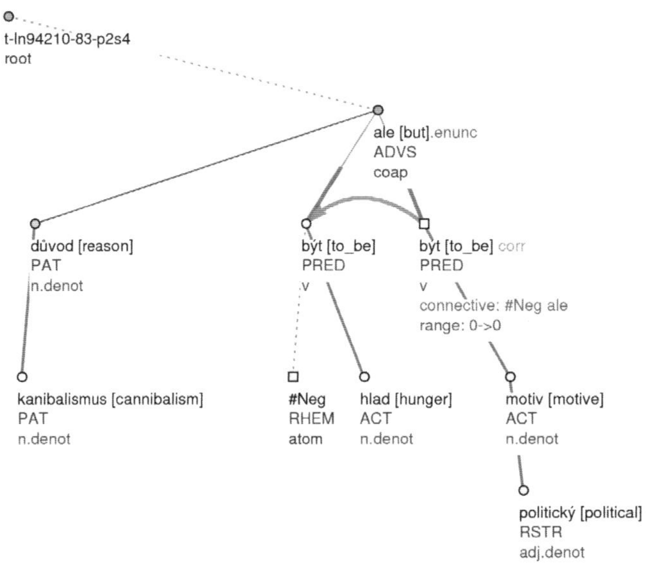

FIGURE 2 – An example of an intra-sentential discourse relation annotated during the first phase

1.2.1 Step 1: Manual Annotation (Mostly of the Inter-Sentential Relations)

The first phase of the annotation was a thorough manual processing of the treebank primarily focused on the inter-sentential relations (relations between sentences) signalled by explicit discourse connectives. Example 1 and Figure 1 show an inter-sentential discourse relation of type *opposition* with explicit connective *ale* (*but*).

(1) *Lidé chtějí platit jen to, co skutečně spotřebovali.*
Ještě dlouho tomu tak ***ale*** *patrně nebude.*

People only want to pay for what they really consumed.
But *apparently, it will not be so yet for a long time.*

Intra-sentential relations (within a sentence) were during the first phase only marked manually in cases where the discourse type could not be determined unambiguously by the tectogrammatical label (functor) and the actual discourse type was not prevailing for the given functor. For instance, the tectogrammatical label (functor) ADVS (the *adversative* relation, in our case clausal) is too general and corresponds to several finer discourse types, namely the types of *opposition*, *restrictive opposition*, *correction*, *confrontation*, and *concession*. *Opposition* is predominant among the discourse types for the functor ADVS, so it was not annotated in the first phase (and was left for the second phase)[7]. All the other discourse types for the functor ADVS were annotated manually in the first phase. The situation is illustrated by Example 2 and Figure 2; on the tectogrammatical layer, the relation between the two clauses was labelled as ADVS

[7] See Table 1 for predominant discourse types for various functors.

(functor of the coordinative node in Figure 2); the discourse type is *correction* (the relation is marked by the arrow with label *corr* in Figure 2).

(2) *Důvodem kanibalismu nebyl hlad, **ale** politické motivy.*

*The reason for the cannibalism was not hunger **but** political motives.*

For a more detailed description of the manual annotation of the treebank including the annotation evaluation see e.g. Jínová et al. 2012.

1.2.2 Step 2: Automatic Annotation of the Intra-Sentential Relations

The second phase of the annotations consisted predominantly of an automatic procedure that extracted mostly tectogrammatical features and used them directly for the annotation of intra-sentential discourse relations. The main goal was to find and mark all so far unmarked intra-sentential discourse relations.

This is the main topic of the present paper and we describe it in detail in the following sections. Section 2 briefly describes the manual preparatory work preceding the automated part of the extraction. Section 3 is devoted to the automatic annotation itself and to some practical issues connected to it. In Section 4, we mention two necessary manual corrections performed after the automatic annotation, and we evaluate our results in Section 5, which is followed by a conclusion.

2 Pre-Annotation

Two manual steps preceded the automatic annotation of the intra-sentential discourse relations: completely manually annotated selected intra-sentential relations and partially manually annotated temporal relations.

2.1 Manual Work

As explained in Subsection 1.2.1 (Example 2, Figure 2), some of the intra-sentential discourse relations were annotated manually during the first phase of the annotations. It was 510 vertical (subordinate) relations and 1,681 horizontal (coordinate)[8] intra-sentential relations. Other cases of intra-sentential relations, where the tectogrammatical annotation was adequate for the discourse interpretation, were left to the second phase. As an example, if we follow the sub-classification of the ADVS tectogrammatical label for discourse semantics mentioned above in 1.2.1, except for the relations marked previously in the manual phase, the remaining cases were all automatically set to discourse type *opposition (opp)*, see Table 1 and Section 3.1 for details.

2.2 Semi-Automatic Annotation

Finite verbs with the type of dependency being one of the temporal relations (functors TFHL, THL, THO, TSIN, TTILL, TWHEN) were pre-processed manually. For each of

[8] In dependency trees of PDT, root nodes of coordinated phrases are captured as siblings (direct children of the coordinating node), hence "horizontal" relations.

them, the type of the discourse relation was set by a human annotator, along with the direction of the relation (whether from the dependent node to its governor or the other way)[9] and the exact position of the arguments (the nodes themselves or possibly their coordinating nodes (if present)). All this information was annotated in a table and passed to the automatic script to create the discourse relations and to find and set the appropriate connective to each relation automatically. Altogether, it was 491 relations.

3 Automatic Annotation

After the manual annotation described in Subsection 2.1 and the manual preprocessing of temporal relations described in Subsection 2.2, an automatic script went through the tectogrammatical layer of the whole data of PDT, document by document, sentence by sentence and node by node.

If the node represented

- a finite verb with one of the temporal functors (TFHL, THL, THO, TSIN, TTILL, TWHEN), it was annotated using the information from the manually created table (Subsection 2.2 above).
- a finite verb with functor CAUS, COND, CNCS, AIM, CONTRD or SUBS, it became a candidate for an automatically detected vertical discourse relation.
- a coordination node with functor REAS, CSQ, ADVS, CONFR, GRAD, CONJ or DISJ, coordinating (directly or transitively) finite verbs or non-finite-verbal nodes with functor PRED[10], it became a candidate for a horizontal relation.

In all cases, the connective was detected automatically (see below in Subsection 3.4).

Vertical Relations

Candidates for a vertical relation were checked for a presence of a previously manually annotated relation; if there was none, an automatic discourse relation was created, in the basic case directly between the dependant and governing verbal nodes. If one of the nodes was a member of a coordination, more complex procedure was used to set the exact position of the arguments (see below Subsections 3.2 and 3.2.1). The discourse type and direction of the discourse arrow were set based on the tectogrammatical functor of the dependant node, see Subsection 3.1 below for details. Finally, the connective was found and set – see Subsection 3.4 for the procedure.

Horizontal Relations

Similarly, candidates for a horizontal relation were checked for a presence of a previously manually annotated relation; if there was none, an automatic discourse

[9] There is a rich variety of connectives, and also verbal aspect values and negation play a role. These features in combination determine the discourse type and also the direction of the discourse arrow (i.e. the nature of the discourse arguments: *precedence – succession*). However, as the occurrences in the data were not so many, it was faster to decide on the type of the relation and the order of arguments manually.

[10] PRED – a tectogrammatical predicate; for a list and description of all functors, please see the tectogrammatical manual: http://ufal.mff.cuni.cz/pdt2.0/doc/manuals/en/t-layer/html/ch07.html

relation was created among the members of the coordination. A special case of multiple coordinations is discussed in 3.2.2 below. The discourse type and direction of the arrow were established based on the tectogrammatical functor of the coordinating node, again see Subsection 3.1 below for details. Subsection 3.4 describes the procedure of searching for the connective of the horizontal relation.

3.1 Functor to Discourse Type Conversion

Table 1 shows a list of tectogrammatical functors and their corresponding prevailing discourse types. After the manual annotation, the table could be (and was) used to identify the discourse type of the remaining relations. Note that it is still not a 1-1 relation, for example the discourse type *confrontation* can be signalled by two different functors (CONTRD and CONFR), as we give up the syntactic distinction of hypotactic (CONTRD) vs. paratactic (CONFR) in this respect. The transformation table was used for all automatically annotated horizontal relations (7,392 cases) and all automatically annotated vertical relations (2,599 cases).

Functor	**Functor (long name)**[11]	**Discourse type**	**Discourse type (long name)**
AIM	purpose	purp	purpose
CAUS	cause	reason	reason-result
CNCS	concession	conc	concession
COND	condition	cond	condition
CONTRD	confrontation	confr	confrontation
SUBS	substitution	corr	correction
ADVS	adversative relation	opp	opposition
CONFR	confrontation	confr	confrontation
CONJ	conjunction	conj	conjunction
CSQ	consequence	reason	reason-result
DISJ	disjunction	disjalt	disjunctive alternative
GRAD	gradation	grad	gradation
REAS	causal relation	reason	reason-result

TABLE 1 – Functor to discourse type automatic translation table; the first six rows represent vertical relations, the last seven rows represent horizontal relations.

3.2 Arguments with Coordinations

In PDT, coordinating expressions are represented as separate nodes and technically they are not different from other nodes representing content words. In the detection of discourse arguments, two situations needed to be treated in a special way, as described in the following two subsections.

[11] taken from the tectogrammatical manual: http://ufal.mff.cuni.cz/pdt2.0/doc/manuals/en/t-layer/html/ch07.html

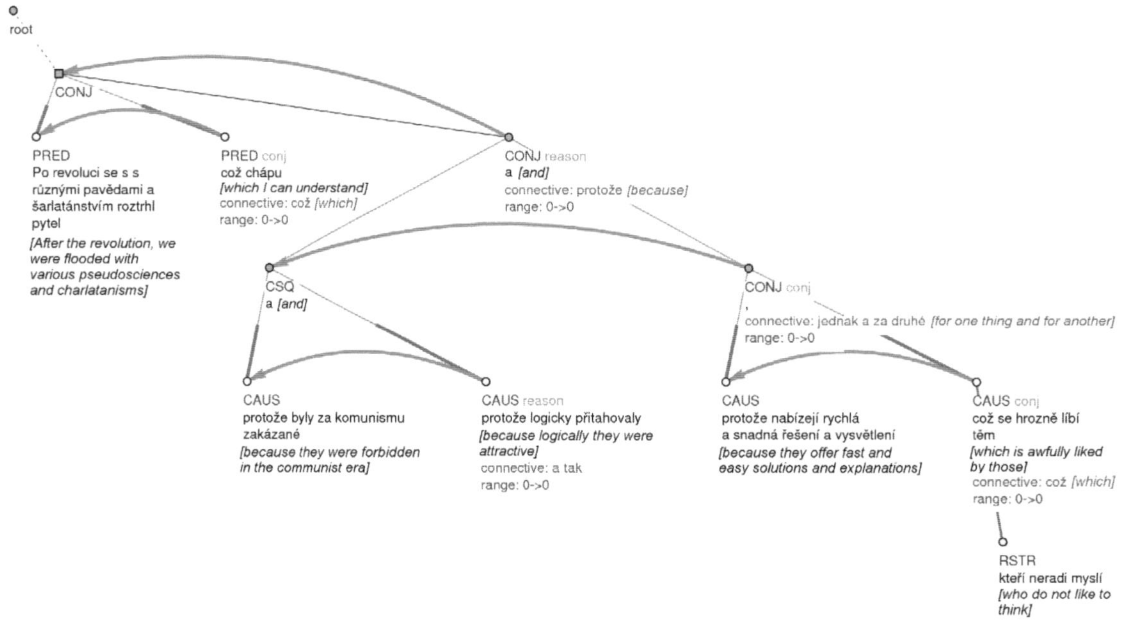

FIGURE 3 – An example of mixed coordinations in a folded mode.

3.2.1 Coordinated Structures in the Detection of the Argument Position

In many cases, an argument of a discourse relation is represented by a coordination of verbal nodes, not by the verbal nodes individually. In such cases, the position of the argument was shifted from the verbal nodes to the coordinating node. It could even happen transitively, so the topmost suitable coordination was always searched for.

Example 3 demonstrates a complex case of coordinated arguments. The situation is depicted in Figure 3, which is a tectogrammatical tree in a folded mode (nodes of the tree represent individual clauses or coordinations)[12]. All discourse annotation in the tree is a result of the automatic procedure.

(3) *Po revoluci se s různými pavědami a šarlatánstvím roztrhl pytel,* ***což*** *chápu,* ***protože jednak*** *byly za komunismu zakázané,* ***a tak*** *logicky přitahovaly,* ***a za druhé*** *nabízejí rychlá a snadná řešení a vysvětlení,* ***což*** *se hrozně líbí těm, kteří neradi myslí.*

After the revolution, we were flooded with various pseudosciences and charlatanisms, ***which*** *I can understand,* ***because for one thing****, they were forbidden in the communist era* ***and so*** *logically they were attractive,* ***and for another****, they offer fast and easy solutions and explanations,* ***which*** *is awfully liked by those who do not like to think.*

[12] For all features of the annotation tool for discourse, see Mírovský et al. (2010).

In this example sentence, five discourse relations along with their types and connectives have been automatically detected. Four of them are horizontal relations:

i. a horizontal relation of type *conj* between clauses *"Po revoluci se ... roztrhl pytel"* (*"After the revolution, we were flooded ... charlatanisms"*), and *"chápu"* (*"I can understand"*), with the connective *což* (*which*),

ii. a horizontal relation of type *reason* between clauses *"logicky přitahovaly"* (*"logically they were attractive"*) and *"byly za komunismu zakázané"* (*"they were forbidden in the communist era"*), with the connective *"a tak"* (*"and so"*),

iii. a horizontal relation of type *conj* between clauses *"nabízejí ... vysvětlení"* (*"they offer ... explanations"*) and *"se hrozně líbí ... neradi myslí"* (*"is awfully liked ... do not like to think"*), with the connective *což* (*which*),

iv. and a horizontal relation of type *conj* between coordinations of clauses in (ii) and (iii), with the connective *"jednak a za druhé"* (*"for one thing and for another"*).

One of them is a vertical relation:

v. a vertical relation of type *reason* between the coordination of the coordinations in (iv) and the coordination of clauses in (i), with the connective *protože* (*because*).

Cases (i), (ii) and (iii) are simple cases where the arguments are represented directly by the coordinated verbal nodes.

Case (iv) is also a relatively simple case, only a presence of a coordinated[13] finite-verb in the subtree of both the coordinated clauses needed to be checked (transitively in general).

Case (v) is a vertical discourse relation represented by an arrow between the two coordinating nodes. The relation was however signalled by four occurrences of functor CAUS, marking a linguistic (effective) dependency[14] between each of the transitively coordinated finite verbs with this functor[15] and each of their linguistic parents (finite verbs *"roztrhnout se"* (*"be flooded"*) and *chápat* (*"to understand"*)), which are also coordinated. The arguments of the relation(s) needed to be lifted to the topmost suitable coordinating nodes.[16] Thus, instead of eight discourse relations that could be created directly between the individual verbal nodes, only one overall discourse relation was created, which is a more comprehensible solution, without a loss of any information.

In all detected vertical relations, the effective parent was shifted by one coordination level 263 times, resulting in 110 discourse relations, and by two coordination levels 8 times, resulting in 3 discourse relations. The effective child was shifted by one

[13] The tectogrammatical attribute is_member serves to distinguishing coordinated and non-coordinated children of a coordinating node.

[14] The effective dependency is a linguistic dependency between nodes representing content words, taking all effects of coordinations etc. into account.

[15] verbal nodes *"být (zakázaný)"* (*"to be (forbidden)"*), *přitahovat* (*"to be attractive"*), *nabízet* (*"to offer"*), and *"líbit se"* (*"to be liked"*)

[16] Again, the tectogrammatical attribute is_member was used.

coordination level 634 times, resulting in 314 discourse relations, and by two coordination levels 61 times, resulting in 25 discourse relations.

3.2.2 Multiple Coordinations

In case of multiple coordinations (coordinations with more than two members) with only a comma as the conjunction of the first members of the coordination and a connective (often *a* (*and*)) as the conjunction of the last two members of the coordination, only the last two members form a discourse relation with an explicit connective (as we do not consider a comma to be a discourse connective). Example 4 demonstrates such a case:

(4) *Pozoroval jsem jednou jednu slečnu: seděla u PC, měla prst zabořen do klávesnice* ***a*** *evidentně se nudila.*

I watched a young lady once: she was sitting at a PC, had her finger buried in the keyboard ***and*** *evidently was bored.*[17]

Here, a discourse relation was only created between clauses "*evidentně se nudila*" ("*evidently was bored*") and "*měla prst zabořen do klávesnice*" ("*had her finger buried in the keyboard*"), with *a* (*and*) as a connective. The other discourse relations in these coordinations are considered implicit and will be annotated in the future, during the annotations of implicit discourse relations.

Multiple coordinations of this type occur 501 times in the data.

3.3 Scope of Arguments

In all intra-sentential relations, the scope of a discourse argument is defined as the effective subtree[18] of the root node of the argument (the root node of the argument can either be a finite verb or a node coordinating[19] finite verbs or another type of node with functor PRED), excluding all nodes of the other argument of the relation. In all 10,482 automatically annotated intra-sentential relations, the tectogrammatical tree structure correctly defined the scope of the arguments, independently of the fact whether the argument was formed on the surface by a continuous sequence of words or not.[20]

3.4 Detection of Discourse Connectives

In most cases, the discourse connectives of intra-sentential discourse relations could be automatically detected on the basis of the information on the tectogrammatical and analytical layers.

---

[17] The presence of a subject in a Czech clause is irrelevant for the decision whether to annotate a discourse relation or not, as Czech is a pro-drop language. Hence, the English translation of the example sentence with no subject in the last two clauses is not to be treated as a VP coordination, which would not be annotated in some projects for English like the PDTB (see Prasad, 2007)

[18] Effective subtree of a node is a set of nodes that linguistically depend (transitively) on the given node, taking all effects of coordinations etc. into account.

[19] possibly transitively, i.e. through other coordinating nodes

[20] For the 2,191 manually annotated intra-sentential relations, in all but 146 cases the scope of arguments was also equal to the effective subtree of the root node, in the 146 cases the annotator had to define a different scope of the argument.

Connectives of the vertical relations can be found among nodes from the analytical layer that correspond to the verbal root of the discourse argument on the tectogrammatical layer. All auxiliary analytical counterparts (not the lexical counterpart) of the verbal node except for auxiliary verbs and reflexive particles (*se*, *si*) become a part of the connective.

Connectives of the horizontal relations can be found on the tectogrammatical layer at the coordinating node (all its analytical counterparts, e.g. *a* (*and*), *buď* – *nebo* (*either* – *or*), etc.) or its modifiers (functor CM (conjunction modifier), e.g. *dokonce* (*even*), *přesto* (*despite of that*), or negation).

With the exception of 23 atypical cases (which were fixed manually, see Subsection 4.1), discourse connectives could be detected automatically for all 10,482 intra-sentential discourse relations. In the rest of this subsection, we point out three special cases of the connective detection.

3.4.1 Connectives with *tak*, *pak*, *potom*

For vertical relation, connectives like *jestliže* – *pak* (*if* – *then*), the second part (*pak* (*then*)) needed to be found among the effective children of the effective parent(s) of the given verbal node. They were filtered using the tectogrammatical lemma (only *tak, pak, potom* (*so, then, then*)) and the functor (only PREC or one of the temporal relations). It happened 93 times in the data.

3.4.2 Connectives with Expression *což*

The expression *což* (*which*) can represent an intra-sentential connective with the *conjunctive* meaning even though it can be inflected and plays a role of a participant of the clause structure (including a valence participant). To make it possible to distinguish the connective role of this expression automatically, grammatical coreference[21] was used. If the annotated anaphoric link from the expression *což* referred to the coordinated verbal phrase (or in a more complex case to a coordination of verbal phrases), *což* became a part of the connective. See Example 5, where *což* (*which*) refers (via the grammatical coreference) to *stal se* (*became*):

(5) *Pavlov se pak stal předsedou vlády,* ***což*** *se Klausovi přihodilo nakonec také.*

Pavlov then became the prime minister, ***which*** *after all happened to Klaus as well.*

In the data, 220 occurrences of the expression *což* have a grammatical coreference link to a finite-verb node, 11 occurrences have this link to a coordination of finite-verb nodes. Altogether, 231 discourse relations were created with *což* (*which*) as a part of the connective.

[21] Grammatical coreference was annotated in PDT for expressions where it is possible to identify the coreferred part of the text on the basis of grammatical rules (see Mikulová et. al, 2005).

3.4.3 Double Connectives

In some cases of a vertical relation where dependant finite verbal nodes are coordinated, the coordinated clauses begin with separate or different connectives, like *protože – protože* (*because – because*) in Example 6. Both the connectives become a part of the connective of the discourse relation.

(6) *... je škodlivý a ideologicky zavádějící,* ***protože*** *odráží nedůvěru v racionalitu chování každého z nás a* ***protože*** *implikuje falešnou víru ve schopnosti některých z nás vytvořit pro nás ostatní lepší, dokonalejší svět.*

... is harmful and ideologically misleading ***because*** *it reflects the mistrust in the behaviour rationality of each of us and* ***because*** *it implicates a false faith in the ability of some of us to create for the rest of us a better, more perfect world.*

This happened 69 times in our data.

4 Manual Corrections

After the automatic annotation, a few manual checks and corrections were needed. They are described in the following two subsections.

4.1 Failures in the Connective Identification

After having run the script, some manual correction turned up to be necessary in cases where the automatic search for connectives failed (23 cases in sum). These failures arose from two types of situation. First, connectives were placed on a non-typical position in the tree. Second, connectives were not present in the sentence at all. This situation is illustrated by Example 7: the last clause (*he did not pay for this*) is interpreted as a causal sentence on the tectogrammatical layer, but no connective signals this relation.

(7) *... vůbec nejhorší posádka v safari busu je smíšená: Angličan si zapomene kameru v hotelu a chce se vrátit, Francouz zuří, za tohle neplatil!*

... the absolutely worst crew in a safari bus is a mixed one: the Englishman forgets his camera in the hotel and wants to go back, the Frenchman is furious, he did not pay for this!

In the first type of situation, the connective was added manually (we count these relations under the manually annotated ones), in the second type (as in Example 7), the whole relation was deleted for violation of the surface-present connective rule.

4.2 Clauses Depending on a Noun Phrase or an Infinitive

Solely manual treatment required those types of constructions where the dependent clause with discourse semantics was related to a complex predicate structure containing a noun phrase or an infinitive. Only semantics allows to distinguish cases where the dependent clause is related to the whole predicate structure from those related only to an infinitive or a noun phrase. Consider Examples 8 and 9. In both structures, the dependent clause is a child-node of the infinitive, but only in Example 8 it is semantically related to the whole predicate structure *"je ochoten povolit"* (*"is willing to permit"*). In Example 9 the dependent clause is semantically related only to the noun phrase *"připravenost odpovědět silou"* (*"readiness to respond with force"*). As we only annotate discourse relations between text spans with finite verbs, only in Example 8 a discourse relation was annotated.

(8) *Srbský prezident Slobodan Miloševič je ochoten povolit mezinárodní kontrolu své blokády bosenských Srbů,* ***pokud*** *bude obdobná kontrola uplatněna i na hranicích Chorvatska a Bosny.*

The Serbian president Slobodan Milosevic is willing to permit an international inspection of his blockade of the Bosnian Serbs ***if*** *a similar control is applied also on borders of Croatia and Bosnia.*

(9) *Zdůraznili však také připravenost odpovědět silou,* ***pokud*** *opozice bude trvat na použití zbraní.*

However, they also emphasised their readiness to respond with force ***if*** *the opposition will insist on the use of weapons.*

There were 146 cases with such a dependent clause related to the whole predicate structure and 73 occurrences where it was not the case.

5 Summary

Table 2 shows the summary of all relations annotated during both phases of the project, and gives detailed numbers of various "types" of the intra-sentential relations. The last row of the table presents the whole number of all annotated discourse relations of any type.[22]

Type of the relation	count
Intra-sentential relations	12,673
- automatic vertical	2,599
- semi-automatic vertical	491
- automatic horizontal	7,392
- manual vertical	510
- manual horizontal	1,681
Inter-sentential (all manual)	5,514
Total	18,187

TABLE 2 – Overview of discourse relations annotated in PDT

We were able to automatically convert 9,991 (2,599 vertical and 7,392 horizontal) tectogrammatical dependencies into discourse relations, along with all properties of the relations (i.e. the position of arguments, the discourse type and the connective). For

[22] Let us emphasize again: although everything was done on the whole PDT data, all reported numbers only refer to the training and development test parts of the data (9/10 of the treebank, 43,955 sentences).

another 491 vertical dependencies, the discourse type, the order of arguments and their position according to possible coordinations were set manually, as explained in Subsection 2.2, while the rest of the work with these relations was also done automatically; we count these relations as semi-automatic. Mostly during the first phase of the annotation, 2,191 (510 vertical and 1,681 horizontal) intra-sentential discourse relations were annotated completely manually. After the automatic procedure, non-typical connectives needed to be fixed in 23 cases, and 146 relations between a dependent clause and a complex predicate structure needed to be manually added, as explained in Section 4.

Conclusion

In the paper, we have presented in detail the second phase of the discourse annotation project in the Prague Dependency Treebank 2.5, namely the semi-automatic annotation of intra-sentential discourse relations marked by an explicit connective. In the preceding first phase of the project, the whole treebank was processed manually and all inter-sentential relations were marked by a human annotator. Also all intra-sentential relations were assessed manually and those relations whose discourse semantics was not unambiguously inferable from the tectogrammatical information were annotated. After the manual annotation, the tectogrammatical interpretation of the remaining relations conveyed the discourse semantics properly and, in the second phase of the project, all these remaining intra-sentential relations were annotated semi-automatically or automatically. During the automatic part of the annotation, the presence of a discourse relation, the exact position of its arguments, its discourse type and the connective were automatically detected, using the annotation of the deep-syntax dependency trees at the tectogrammatical layer of PDT. As a final step, a few manual checks and corrections were performed.

We have also discussed interesting theoretical observations revealed during the semi-automatic annotation, namely to what extent a syntax-based discourse analysis is automatically processible and what are the special (and so linguistically interesting) cases that require more attention.

The annotated data (both intra- and inter-sentential relations) was published in the autumn of 2012 under the same licence as the underlying PDT 2.5, i.e. the Creative Commons licence[23]. It is available (downloadable) from the repository of LINDAT-Clarin – Centre for Language Research Infrastructure in the Czech Republic[24].

Acknowledgments

We gratefully acknowledge support from the Grant Agency of the Czech Republic (grants P406/12/0658 and P406/2010/0875) and from the Ministry of Education, Youth and Sports in the Czech Republic, program KONTAKT (ME10018) and the LINDAT-Clarin project (LM2010013).

[23] http://creativecommons.org
[24] http://www.lindat.cz

References

Al-Saif, A; Markert, K. (2010). The Leeds Arabic Discourse Treebank: Annotating discourse connectives for Arabic. In *Proceedings of the 7th International Conference on Language Resources and Evaluation (LREC 2010)*, Valletta, Malta, pp. 2046–2053.

Bejček, E., Panevová, J., Popelka, J., Smejkalová, L., Straňák, P., Ševčíková, M., Štěpánek, J., Toman, J., Žabokrtský, Z., Hajič, J. (2012). Prague Dependency Treebank 2.5. *Data/software, Charles University in Prague,* Czech Republic, http://ufal.mff.cuni.cz/pdt2.5/.

Carlson, L., Marcu, D., and Okurowski, M.E. (2002). *RST Discourse Treebank,* LDC2002T07 [Corpus]. Linguistic Data Consortium, Philadelphia, PA, USA.

Hajič, J., Panevová, J., Hajičová, E., Sgall, P., Pajas, P., Štěpánek, J., Havelka, J., Mikulová, M., Žabokrtský, Z. and Ševčíková-Razímová, M. (2006). *Prague Dependency Treebank 2.0.* Software prototype, Linguistic Data Consortium, Philadelphia, PA, USA, ISBN 1-58563-370-4, www.ldc.upenn.edu, Jul 2006.

Mírovský, J., Jínová, P., Poláková, L. (2012). Does Tectogrammatics help the Annotation of Discourse? In *Procedings of the 24th International Conference on Computational Linguistics (COLING 2012)*, Mumbai, India, December 2012.

Jínová, P., Mírovský, J., Poláková, L. (2012). Analyzing the Most Common Errors in the Discourse Annotation of the Prague Dependency Treebank. In *Proceedings of the 11th International Workshop on Treebanks and Linguistic Theories (TLT 11),* Lisboa, Portugal.

Mikulová, M., Bémová, A., Hajič, J., Hajičová, E., Havelka, J., Kolářová-Řezníčková, V., Kučová, L., Lopatková, M., Pajas, P., Panevová, J., Razímová, M., Sgall, P., Štěpánek, J., Urešová, Z., Veselá, K. and Žabokrtský, Z. (2005). *Anotace na tektogramatické rovině Pražského závislostního korpusu. Anotátorská příručka.* Praha: UFAL MFF. Available at: http://ufal.mff.cuni.cz/pdt2.0/doc/manuals/cz/t-layer/html/index.html.

Mírovský, J., Mladová, L., Žabokrtský, Z. (2010). Annotation Tool for Discourse in PDT. In *Proceedings of the 23rd International Conference on Computational Linguistics (Coling 2010)*, Beijing, China, pp. 9-12.

Prasad, R., Dinesh, N., Lee, A., Miltsakaki, E., Robaldo, L., Joshi, A. and Webber, B. (2007). *The Penn Discourse TreeBank 2.0 Annotation Manual.* Available at: http://www.seas.upenn.edu/~pdtb/PDTBAPI/pdtb-annotation-manual.pdf.

Prasad, R., Dinesh, N., Lee, A., Miltsakaki, E., Robaldo, L., Joshi, A. and Webber, B. (2008). The Penn Discourse Treebank 2.0. In *Proceedings of the 6th International Conference on Language Resources and Evaluation (LREC 2008), Marrakech, Morocco, pp. 2961–2968.*

Sgall, P., Hajičová, E. and Panevová, J. (1986). *The Meaning of the Sentence in Its Semantic and Pragmatic Aspects,* Praha: Academia.

Zeyrek, D., Demirşahin Işın, Çallı A. B. S., Balaban H. Ö., Yalçınkaya İ., & Turan Ü. D. (2010). The annotation scheme of the Turkish Discourse Bank and an evaluation of inconsistent annotations. In *Proceedings of the Fourth Linguistic Annotation Workshop, ACL 2010*, Uppsala, Sweden, pp. 282–289.

Yuping Zhou and Nianwen Xue. (2012). PDTB-style discourse annotation of Chinese text. In *Proceedings of the 50th Annual Meeting of the Association for Computational Linguistics (ACL 2012),* Jeju, Republic of Korea, pp. 69–77.

Incremental Construction of Robust but Deep Semantic Representations for Use in Responsive Dialogue Systems

Andreas PELDSZUS[1] *David SCHLANGEN*[2]
(1) Department of Linguistics, Potsdam University, Germany
(2) Faculty of Linguistics and Literary Studies, Bielefeld University, Germany
`peldszus@uni-potsdam.de, david.schlangen@uni-bielefeld.de`

ABSTRACT
It is widely acknowledged that current dialogue systems are held back by a lack of flexibility, both in their turn-taking model (typically, allowing only a strict back-and-forth between user and system) and in their interpretation capabilities (typically, restricted to slot filling). We have developed a component for NLU that attempts to address both of these challenges, by a) constructing *robust but deep meaning representations* that support a range of further user intention determination techniques from inference / reasoning-based ones to ones based on more basic structures, and b) constructing these representations *incrementally* and hence providing semantic information on which system reactions can be based concurrently to the ongoing user utterance. The approach is based on an existing semantic representation formalism, Robust Minimal Recursion Semantics, which we have modified to suit incremental construction. We present the modifications, our implementation, and discuss applications within a dialogue system context, showing that the approach indeed promises to meet the requirements for more flexibility.

KEYWORDS: Incremental Processing, Semantics Construction, Dialogue Systems, Dialogue, Natural Language Understanding, Spoken Language.

Proceedings of the Workshop on Advances in Discourse Analysis and its Computational Aspects (ADACA), pages 59–76,
COLING 2012, Mumbai, December 2012.

1 Introduction

To advance beyond the domains that currently are covered by spoken dialogue systems—acquisition of information for database queries—into more collaborative domains such as explored in the pioneering work by Allen *et al.* (Allen et al., 1995; Ferguson and Allen, 1998), progress in at least three areas will be required. First, as is well known in the study of conversational behaviour, collaboration extends to the contruction of the dialogue contributions themselves (Clark, 1996), something that is precluded by the strict back-and-forth turn-taking model of current dialogue systems. Second, less clearly scripted (and scriptable) domains require deeper interpretation of contributions (Allen et al., 2005). Finally, the problems of coverage that the deep representation-based BDI (beliefs, desires, intentions) approach ran into (discussed for example in (Jurafsky, 2003)) suggest that complementary principled reasoning mechanisms such as recently explored in the field of Artificial Intelligence (e.g., (Domingos et al., 2006; Zettlemoyer et al., 2009)) will need to be applied.

The first of these areas, more flexible turn-taking through incremental processing, has received much attention recently (Aist et al., 2007; Skantze and Schlangen, 2009; Baumann et al., 2009; Buß and Schlangen, 2010; Skantze and Hjalmarsson, 2010; DeVault et al., 2011), and has shown improvements in the perceived naturalness of the resulting systems. However, the implemented systems still followed the simpler information-transaction model, and used shallow meaning representations. In this paper, we present our work towards connecting attempts to improve such temporal flexibilty with the use of deeper representations.

We base our work on an existing semantic representation formalism (RMRS, (Copestake, 2006)) that is designed to capture as much or as little semantic information as could be recovered from an input. Hence, even though it has previously only been used in the much different application of monological information extraction (Schäfer, 2007), this formalism fits well the requirement of robustness for spoken dialogue systems, where input to interpretation may be deviant from standard syntax both in actual fact, through speech disfluency, as well as practically, because of speech recognition problems. We modify this formalism so that it is suitable for incremental semantic construction (Section 4). We present our implementation that combines incremental semantic construction with top-down incremental parsing (Section 5), and describe how we have applied it in applications that begin to make use of hybrid reasoning techniques (Section 6).

2 Related Work

Incremental semantic construction has been tackled occasionally in the literature. As mentioned in the introduction, many of the extant approaches represent meaning in domain-specific semantic frames which are then filled incrementally, often using shallow probabilistic models (see e.g. (Sagae et al., 2009; Heintze et al., 2010)). As our focus in this work is on providing deep representations, the more relevant work is that taking a theoretical, linguistic perspective.

The Dynamic Syntax (DS) grammar formalism (Kempson et al., 2001), for example, presents an incremental parsing-directed approach to semantic construction. Instead of using syntactic trees, the grammar here is mainly specified by lexical actions that directly build a propositional tree. DS offers sophisticated syntax-semantic theorizing and models ellipsis and anaphora phenomena. Recently DS has been applied to sequences of dialog utterances (Gargett et al., 2009); a first outline of a dialog system implementing DS has been presented by Purver et al. (2011). However, coming from a theoretical linguistics background, the approach still centers around notions of grammaticality, whereas in practical applications, robustness is perhaps the more important notion. Moreover, DS is somewhat 'monolithic', making it hard to substitute, say, the grammar, the lexicon or the semantic composition by an alternative while keeping the rest. We aim to remain more theory-neutral towards grammar and (base-language) semantics in our approach.

PTT (Poesio and Traum, 1997; Poesio and Rieser, 2010) is another relevant approach; here, use is made of tree adjoining grammars and accompanying semantic rule patterns for construction of representations. The main focus of that theory however seems on the incremental construction of discourse structure and on how that enriches the semantics. The semantic construction is only worked out for small examples, and, to our knowledge, not implemented yet.

The work presented here shares many concerns with that of (Allen et al., 2005). However, again in our re-use of existing formalisms and a more standard base-grammar, we strive for more theory-independence. Moreover, our approaches differ in how underspecification is used (where we allow underspecification of predicate-argument relations) and in the way the methods are applied, as will be described below in Section 6.

In (Peldszus et al., 2012), we have described an application of the work presented in the present paper, where the incremental representations generated by the parser were evaluated against the current environment, providing feedback to the parser about which derivation to expand first, thus improving its accuracy. In (Kennington and Schlangen, 2012), we have used the representations as input to a probabilistic reasoning model. While those papers focus on particular applications within a dialogue processing context (see also the brief discussion below in Section 6), the current paper focusses on the representation and construction in itself, properly developing it out of the tradition of principled syntax / semantics interfaces.

3 Using Underspecification to Represent Meaning Increments

Underspecification of semantic representations was introduced in the 1990s as a means to capture ambiguities—mostly those arising out of quantifier scope—efficiently by letting the syntax/semantics interface leave those semantic aspects unspecified which syntax cannot decide. A variety of formalisms was proposed (*inter alia*, (Reyle, 1993; Bos, 1996; Pinkal, 1996; Deemter and Peters, 1996)) which all realised the same basic idea of letting the grammar produce *descriptions* of so-called *base language* logical formulae. The descriptions themselves are formulae, but in a special, tailor-made language; their models then are the base language formulae that do the normal job of representing meaning. In the discourse theory SDRT (Asher and Lascarides, 2003), an underspecification formalism formed the basis of the interface between compositional semantics and discourse implications; this theory was used in (Schlangen, 2003; Schlangen and Lascarides, 2003) to deal with what could be seen as a restricted case of the current phenomenon, namely intentionally non-sentential dialogue utterances.

Here, we use for the representation of meaning increments (that is, the contributions of new words and syntactic constructions) as well as for the resulting logical forms the formalism *Robust Minimal Recursion Semantics* (Copestake, 2006). In this section, we will first introduce the basic features of this formulism and then argue that it is suitable for describing meaning increments in a principled and well-founded way.

Background: (Robust) Minimal Recursion Semantics Minimal Recursion Semantics (MRS) was originally constructed for semantic underspecification (of scope and other phenomena) (Copestake et al., 2005) and then—with the name gaining an additional "R"—adapted to serve the purposes of semantic representation in heterogeneous situations where the results of shallow and deep semantic parsers need to be integrated into a common representation (Copestake, 2006). To this end almost all relational information contained in a logical form is factored into smaller predications, so that, depending on what's required, a fully specified semantic representation can be made less specific by removing some of its predications or by cutting connections between them, or a shallower semantic representation can be expanded monotonically by enrichring it with further statements or by connecting predications.

As in all semantic underspecification formalisms, representing scopal readings is achieved in RMRS by first splitting the logical form into scope-taking and scope-bearing parts (*elementary predications* in RMRS terminology) and then describing the set of admitted embeddings through *scope constraint* statements. The resulting semantic representation is flat, i.e. it can be represented as a list of elementary predications and scope constraints. Removing a scope constraint expands the set of admitted embeddings, while adding one restricts it.

The distinguishing feature of RMRS in comparison with MRS is its ability to underspecify predicate-argument structure. A predicate expression $pred(x, y, z)$ is decomposed further into the "key" predication and *argument relations* which explicitly express which kind of arguments the predication has. Removing such an explicit argument relation hence underspecifies an argument of a predicate expression, while adding one specifies it. Predicates can thus be introduced into the composition process with different specificity: a predicate can be fully specified with fixed arity, i.e. with a defined number of argument positions, and all its arguments given, as in $pred(x, y, z)$; a predicate can have a fixed arity, but leave some argument positions open, which in our simplified illustration could be represented as e.g. $pred(x, y, ?)$; it could be introduced without fixed arity, as illustrated in $pred(?, \ldots)$; and arguments can be introduced without knowing which predicates they are arguments of, as in $?(x, y)$. It is even possible to a bind an argument to a predicate without knowing exactly which argument position it is supposed to fill.

RMRS has several other useful features. First, the underlying representation language is a first order logic with generalized quantifiers, event semantics and sortal variables – common formal tools of semantic representation. Also, the representations can be related to each other in a transparent way: Two RMRS structures can then be tested for subsumption (Copestake, 2007a), in order to see whether one structure is a less specific variant of the other. If one subsumes the other, the difference between both can be formulated as an RMRS containing all those statements that could monotonically enrich the less specific one to yield the more specific structure. Furthermore, it is semantically well-founded. A model-theoretic semantics for the language of RMRS has for example been given in Koller and Lascarides (2009). Finally, RMRS is used widely, for example in the LinGO English Resource Grammar (Flickinger, 2000), or in the "Heart of Gold"-architecture (Schäfer, 2007) as a common semantic representation. The RASP parser (Briscoe and Carroll, 2002) is one example of a shallow (yet non-incremental) parser with an RMRS interface.

Representing Meaning Increments with Underspecification Why do we see these underspecification techniques as useful for representing the meaning of an ongoing utterance and of the increments that add to it?

First and foremost, a crucial requirement for incremental semantic representation is that it facilitates extensibility in a technically straightforward manner; as explained above, this is fulfilled even by the standard formulation of RMRS. Ongoing utterances then may raise expectations about how they might be concluded. Even if an utterance is yet incomplete, we can have expectations about what kinds of words may come and fill the necessary but yet open positions. On the other hand, even for a syntactically potentially complete utterance, we have to remain open for supplemental phrases or appositions. A semantic formalism is required that can adequately represent such constraints on possible extensions. However, an incoming word does not necessarily have to determine how it relates to the existing utterance. Sometimes lexical increments might add to the ongoing utterance without already making explicit in which way they connect, as e.g. with the attachment of prepositional phrases when adding the preposition. The semantic formalism should be able to underspecify these connections accordingly and to specify them when evidence is available. Finally, we want to represent the incremental state not only of perfectly planned utterances, but of spontanous natural speech. The semantic formalism should thus ideally offer devices to robustly cope with those phenomena.

RMRS meets these representational desiderata. As an example, Figure 1 shows a growing logical form in a scope-less flat first-order logic.

Words	Predicates
den	?(e,?,x,...) def(x)
den winkel	?(e,?,x,...) def(x) bracket(x)
den winkel in	?(e,?,x,...) def(x) bracket(x) in(x,y)
den winkel in der	?(e,?,x,...) def(x) bracket(x) in(x,y) def(y)
den winkel in der dritten	?(e,?,x,...) def(x) bracket(x) in(x,y) def(y) third(y)
den winkel in der dritten reihe	?(e,?,x,...) def(x) bracket(x) in(x,y) def(y) third(y) row(y)
den winkel in der dritten reihe nehmen	take(e,c,x) def(x) bracket(x) in(x,y) def(y) third(y) row(y)

Table 1: Example of logical forms (flattened into scope-less first-order base-language formulae for convenience) incrementally growing for the utterance 'den winkel in der dritten reihe nehmen' (*take the bracket in the third row*)

With every incoming word, the logical form is monotonically enriched, either by adding lexical predicates, by connecting predicates via variable identifications or by specifying underspecified positions. For convenience, we restrict the example to the NP-attachment case; also it should be noted that the base-language logical forms shown in the table correspond to highly factored structures in the RMRS description language. Each of these RMRS structures representing a certain state of the ongoing utterances can be conceived as describing in a well-defined way an infinite set of logical forms that all share a common part (namely, the common lexical prefix).

To give an impression of what the full utterance would look like in the RMRS description language, see example (1). This representation shows elementary predications, argument relations and scope constraints. For a more detailed technical description of the RMRS formalism, we refer the interested reader to (Copestake, 2006).

(1) ℓ_7:a_7:_take(e_7), $\mathsf{ARG}_1(a_7, c)$, $\mathsf{ARG}_2(a_7, x_1)$,
ℓ_1:a_1:def(), $\mathsf{BV}(a_1, x_1)$, $\mathsf{RSTR}(a_1, h_1)$, $\mathsf{BODY}(a_1, h_2)$, $h_1 =_q \ell_2$,
ℓ_2:a_2:_bracket(x_1),
ℓ_3:a_3:_in(e_3), $\mathsf{ARG}_1(a_3, x_1)$, $\mathsf{ARG}_2(a_3, x_4)$,
ℓ_4:a_4:def(), $\mathsf{BV}(a_4, x_4)$, $\mathsf{RSTR}(a_4, h_3)$, $\mathsf{BODY}(a_4, h_4)$, $h_3 =_q \ell_5$,
ℓ_5:a_5:_third(e_5), $\mathsf{ARG}_1(a_5, x_4)$,
ℓ_5:a_6:_row(x_4)

The discussion above has shown how RMRS meets the requirements for representing the content

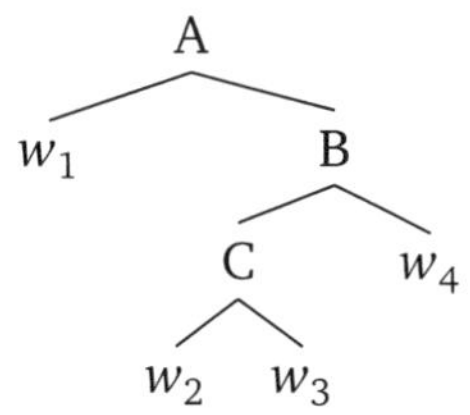

Figure 1: Abstract example tree.

of as-yet (potentially) unfinished utterances. The content that each minimal continuation of an utterance brings with it, *i.e.*, the semantic increment, can be represented in the very same way. We will demonstrate this in the next section.

4 Incremental Semantics Construction in *i*RMRS

After briefly reviewing how standard RMRS deals with semantic construction, we will describe in this section our modifications that enable incremental construction.

Background: Semantics Constructions in RMRS According to Gottlob Frege's principle of compositionality, the meaning of an expression is a result of the meaning of its parts and the way of combination (Frege, 1897). Syntax-driven semantic construction has typically conceived this principle as follows: The decomposition of an expression into parts is determined by the syntactic tree. Each terminal node is assigned a lexical semantics. The rule expanding a non-terminal node identifies the method of combination of that node's daughters' semantics. In order to compute the meaning of the whole expression, the tree is interpreted bottom-up, inside-outside. As an example, consider the abstract tree in Figure 1. To determine the meaning of the whole string, the combination operation determined by node type A has to be applied to the meaning of the first word and to the intermediate meaning result of node B. This is formally represented in Example (2).

(2) $[[w_1 \ldots w_4]] = OP_A([[w_1]], OP_B(OP_C([[w_2]], [[w_3]]), [[w_4]]))$

The semantic algebra proposed for RMRS (Copestake, 2007b) workes pretty much in this way. Syntactic structures are related to operations of semantic combination, as e.g. scopal combination (equivalent to function application) and intersective combination (equivalent to predicate modification). Those operations combine the two RMRS structures "under construction" by joining their list of elementary predications, argument relations and scope constraints. Additionally, as defined by the applied semantic operation, equations between variables of the joined parts relate their semantic representations. Which variables are equated is determined by the so-called "hooks" and "slots", where one structure (the argument) "hooks" into an open "slot" of the other (the functor) to make it semantically more complete. Thus, the semantic representation can grow monotonically at each combinatory step by simply adding predicates, argument relations and scope constraints and by equating variables according to the hook and slot pair.

Formally, hook and slot are triples $[\ell{:}a{:}x]$ consisting of a label for scope underspecification, an anchor for predicate-argument underspecification and an index variable representing the semantic head of the structure. An RMRS can have multiple slots allowing different equations of its variables. To make the subsequent discussion easier, we will call an RMRS under construction *saturated*, if no open slot is left. Statements identifying variables can either enter the structure explicitly, or be immediately resolved with one variable being substituted by the other. We will call an an RMRS under construction *reduced*, if all equalities are resolved. An RMRS under construction corresponds to a normal RMRS, if it is saturated and reduced.

(Copestake, 2007b) describes this process of semantic construction by tree interpretation for two settings: for a lexicalized setting, where the lexical entries already bring a large part of the slot with them (according to their subcategorization scheme), and for a non-lexicalist setting, where the lexical entries are rather generic and all slots are introduced by rule-semantics. We will focus on the latter setting for the rest of this paper.

In both cases, the slots of an RMRS under construction are organised as a bag of named slots. Open slots can be randomly accessed, i.e. independently of the order of slot introduction, if the semantic combination operation identifies it by its name. However, there is the restriction that a slot with a certain name can only exist once in the bag of open slots.

Adaptations for Incremental Construction In an incremental setting, a proper semantic representation is desired for every single state of growth of the syntactic tree. However this is not easily achieved if the order of semantic combination is kept parallel to a bottom-up traversal of the syntactic tree, as assumed in the RMRS semantic algebra. Consider our abstract example in Figure 1 again and suppose that in the current state of the ongoing utterance only the first two words have been uttered. Following a bottom-up combination order, no proper semantic representation could be given for the utterance so far, because the semantic operation associated e.g. with node C requires an argument that is not yet there. One possible solution to this dilemma would be to assign an adequate underspecified semantics to every projected node, in our example for the nodes of w_3 and w_4. Then, the whole tree could be interpreted as described, yielding a proper semantic representation of the ongoing utterance. Unfortunately, the tree will change with the next incoming word, former projected nodes may be specified, new projected nodes may enter the tree. Consequently, the whole process of finding underspecified semantics for open nodes would start again, and not only the new parts of the tree, but the *whole* tree would be required to be interpreted. Because of these two problems, the need to find underspecified semantics for projected nodes and the need for re-interpretation of already existing parts of the tree, we argue that the bottom-up interpretation in this classic form is not adequate for incremental semantic construction.

For our purposes, it is more elegant to proceed with semantic combination in synchronisation with the syntactic expansion of the tree, i.e. in a top-down left-to-right fashion, circumventing the two problems. Consider example (3): The bracketing already makes obvious that the semantic combination is now left-linearized. Every combinatory step yields a semantic representation that can serve as a starting point for the following combinatory step.

(3) $[[w_1 \ldots w_4]] = ((((([[A]] \lhd [[w_1]]) \lhd [[B]]) \lhd [[C]]) \lhd [[w_2]]) \lhd [[w_3]]) \lhd [[w_4]]$

However, in order to define the combination operation signified here with the $\lhd$ symbol, an adjustment to the slot structure of RMRS is required. Left-recursive rules can introduce multiple slots of the same sort before they are filled, which is not allowed in the classic (R)MRS semantic algebra, where only one named slot of each sort can be open at a time. We thus organize the slots as a stack of unnamed slots, where multiple slots of the same sort can be stored, but only the one on top can be accessed. We then define the basic combination operation $\lhd$ equivalent to forward function composition (as in standard lambda calculus, or in CCG (Steedman, 2000)). The basic idea here is the following: When an argument fills the top slot of the functor, the argument's stack of slots itself is pushed onto the functor's stack of slots, so that in the resulting structure the (former) argument's slots get priority over the remaining functor slots. A more formal specification of this operation and our adaptions to RMRS is provided in the appendix for the interested reader.

The stack of semantic slots is thus kept in synchronisation to the stack of syntactic slots. Parallel to the production of syntactic derivations, as the tree is expanded top-down left-to-right, semantic macros are activated for each syntactic rule, composing the contribution of the new increment. If input tokens are matched by the parser, a corresponding generic lexical semantics for that token is added, derived from its lemma and the basic semantic type (individual, event, or underspecified denotations) as determined by its POS tag. This allows for a monotonic semantics construction process that proceeds in lockstep with the syntactic analysis.

A worked example We can now present a small but worked example of the incremental semantic construction process. We directly realize the rule-to-rule hypothesis by annotating every syntactic rule of a toy grammar with a corresponding semantic rule.

For that purpose we first define a few very abstract semantic macros which we call *basic slot manipulators*. None of them contributes an elementary predication or argument relation to the overall representation. Instead they manipulate the slot structure. When the *pop*-combinator $[-]$ is slotted in some RMRS, it merely consumes the top slot without adding anything else; this is required for handling epsilon rules. The *pass*-combinator $[\circ]$ simply restores the slot it has consumed and has no further effect on the representation. It can be seen as a null-semantics and will be the default for any rule without designated rule semantics. The remaining combinators have in common that they add a new slot, besides maintaining the one they have filled. The *equal*-combinator $[=]$ exactly copies the slot, thereby equating labels, anchors and indices, the *plusℓ*-combinator $[+\ell]$ equates labels and indices, and the *plus*-combinator $[+]$ only equates indices. We will use them for modification and adjunction. Note that they are antisymmetric and can be defined for reverse order, e.g. $[\dot{+}]$, depending on the linear order of a node's daughter. Other abstract combinators are possible, but these are the ones we will use frequently.

With those basic semantic macros at hand, we can then define more specific semantic macros to represent the meaning of a syntatic rule. Sometimes rule semantics are just basic macros, in many other cases they add argument relations or even grammar-specific predicates. A specification of some the semantic macros can be found in the appendix.

We will not go very much into detail about the actual execution of all those semantic operations. However, we want to give an impression of the incremental derivation. As an example, consider the utterance "nimm den winkel in...", a simpler version of the example already introduced in Table 1. Its syntactic tree is shown in Figure 2. In Figure 3, we show how the sequence of semantic combinations unfolds corresponding to the syntactic expansion of the tree. We hide the bracketing for convenience and understand the forward slotfilling combination $\lhd$ to be left-associative. The first line shows the ongoing utterance, the second the decomposition according to the syntactic tree, and the third line shows the more or less abstract semantic macros that are successively combined. Remember that all of those macros are RMRSs under construction and that each combinatory step results in a new one, i.e. a proper semantic structure representing the current state of the process is available any time. Also note that we have a clear and transparent description of the semantic increment.

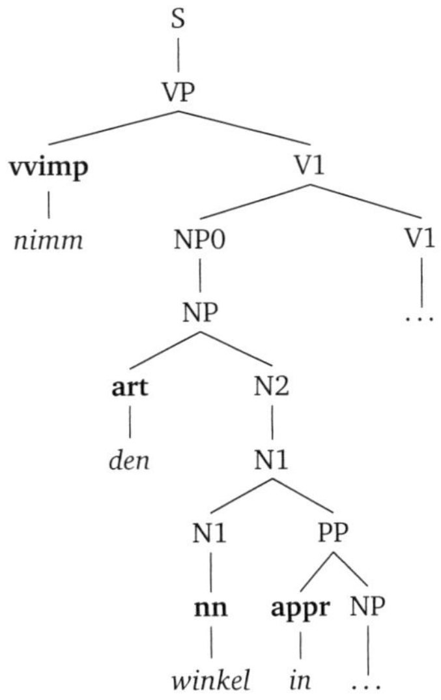

Figure 2: Incremental syntactic derivation of a simple example sentence.

$$[\![\textit{nimm}\dots]\!]$$
$$= [\![\text{S} \rightarrow \text{VP}]\!] \lhd [\![\text{VP} \rightarrow \text{vvimp,V1}]\!] \lhd [\![\textit{nimm}]\!]$$
$$= [\,\circ\,] \lhd [\text{Arg1}] \lhd [\text{adr}] \lhd [=] \lhd [\![\textit{nimm}]\!]$$

$$[\![\textit{nimm den}\dots]\!] = [\![\textit{nimm}\dots]\!] \lhd [\![\textit{den}]\!]$$
$$= \dots \lhd [\![\text{V1} \rightarrow \text{NP0,V1}]\!] \lhd [\![\text{NP0} \rightarrow \text{NP}]\!] \lhd [\![\text{NP} \rightarrow \text{art,N2}]\!] \lhd [\![\textit{den}]\!]$$
$$= \dots \lhd [\text{Arg2}] \lhd [\,\circ\,] \lhd [\text{Q}] \lhd [\![\textit{den}]\!]$$

$$[\![\textit{nimm den winkel}\dots]\!] = [\![\textit{nimm den}\dots]\!] \lhd [\![\textit{winkel}]\!]$$
$$= \dots \lhd [\![\text{N2} \rightarrow \text{N1}]\!] \lhd [\![\text{N1} \rightarrow \text{N1,PP}]\!] \lhd [\![\text{N1} \rightarrow \text{nn}]\!] \lhd [\![\textit{winkel}]\!]$$
$$= \dots \lhd [\,\circ\,] \lhd [+.] \lhd [\,\circ\,] \lhd [\![\textit{winkel}]\!]$$

$$[\![\textit{nimm den winkel in}\dots]\!] = [\![\textit{nimm den winkel}\dots]\!] \lhd [\![\textit{in}]\!]$$
$$= \dots \lhd [\![\text{PP} \rightarrow \text{appr,NP}]\!] \lhd [\![\textit{in}]\!]$$
$$= \dots \lhd [\text{PP}] \lhd [\![\textit{in}]\!]$$

Figure 3: Incremental semantic derivation of a simple example sentence.

5 Implementation in InproTK$_{iRMRS}$

We have implemented this method of semantic construction in the *incremental processing toolkit* (InproTK) (Baumann and Schlangen, 2012), an open-source framework for developing incremental dialogue systems. It realises the abstract model for incremental processing described in (Schlangen and Skantze, 2009), where this processing is conceptualised as consisting of modules that exchange *incremental units*, minimal bits of input and output, that are chained together to form larger units and also linked across modules to allow for revisions.

As mentioned in the introduction, we aim to be theory-neutral if possible, in order to maintain flexibility in case of new emerging linguistic ressources, or newly adopted domains etc. We thus chose to connect more or less "standard" components: A probabilistic top-down parser, a context-free grammar and a common and well-understood semantic representation.

Parser Our parser is a basic version of the approach endorsed by Roark (2001), who presents a strategy for incremental probabilistic top-down parsing and shows that it can compete with high-coverage bottom-up parsers. One of the reasons Roark gives for choosing a top-down approach is that it enables fully left-connected derivations, where at every processing step new increments directly find their place in the existing structure. This monotonically enriched structure can then serve as a context for incremental language understanding, as the author claims, although this part, which we take up here, is not further developed by Roark (2001). The search-space is reduced by using beam search. Due to probabilistic weighing and grammar-transformations, as e.g. the left factorization of the rules to delay certain structural decisions, left recursion poses no direct threat in such an approach. Roark discusses several different techniques for refining his results, such as e.g. including conditioning functions that manipulate a derivation probability on the basis of local linguistic and lexical information; we have for now only implemented the basic strategy. However, in order to cope with spontanous speech and ASR errors, we added three robust lexical operations: *Insertions* consume the current token without matching it to the top stack item. *Deletions* can "consume" a requested but actually non-existent token. *Repairs* adjust unknown tokens to the requested token. These robust operations have strong penalties on the probability to make sure they will survive in the derivation only in critical situations.

Grammar We developed a small grammar (30 rules) covering a "core syntax" of constructions, tailored towards a particular corpus of instructions in task oriented dialogue. These utterances were collected in a Wizard-of-Oz study in the Pentomino puzzle piece domain (which has been used before for example by (Fernández and Schlangen, 2007; Schlangen et al., 2009)). This grammar is hand-written, with weights set according to intuition and manual semantic annotations. With it, we were able to produce semantic representations for a corpus of over 1600 spontaneous dialogue utterances – both for their manually transcriptions as well as for automatic transcription.[1] Although this grammar serves us as a good starting point to experiment with incrementally constructed semantic representations, this obviously is an area for future work. Fortunately, the grammar could easily be substituted by any other context-free grammar, as e.g. one that is induced from a treebank.

Semantic increments in an IU network In the InproTK every increment is represented as an *incremental unit* (IU), which to connected to other units in a network that grows with

[1] We have however only indirectly rated their quality via their interpretability in context (see Peldszus et al., 2012), and so cannot yet give exact numbers for parser perfomance on its own here.

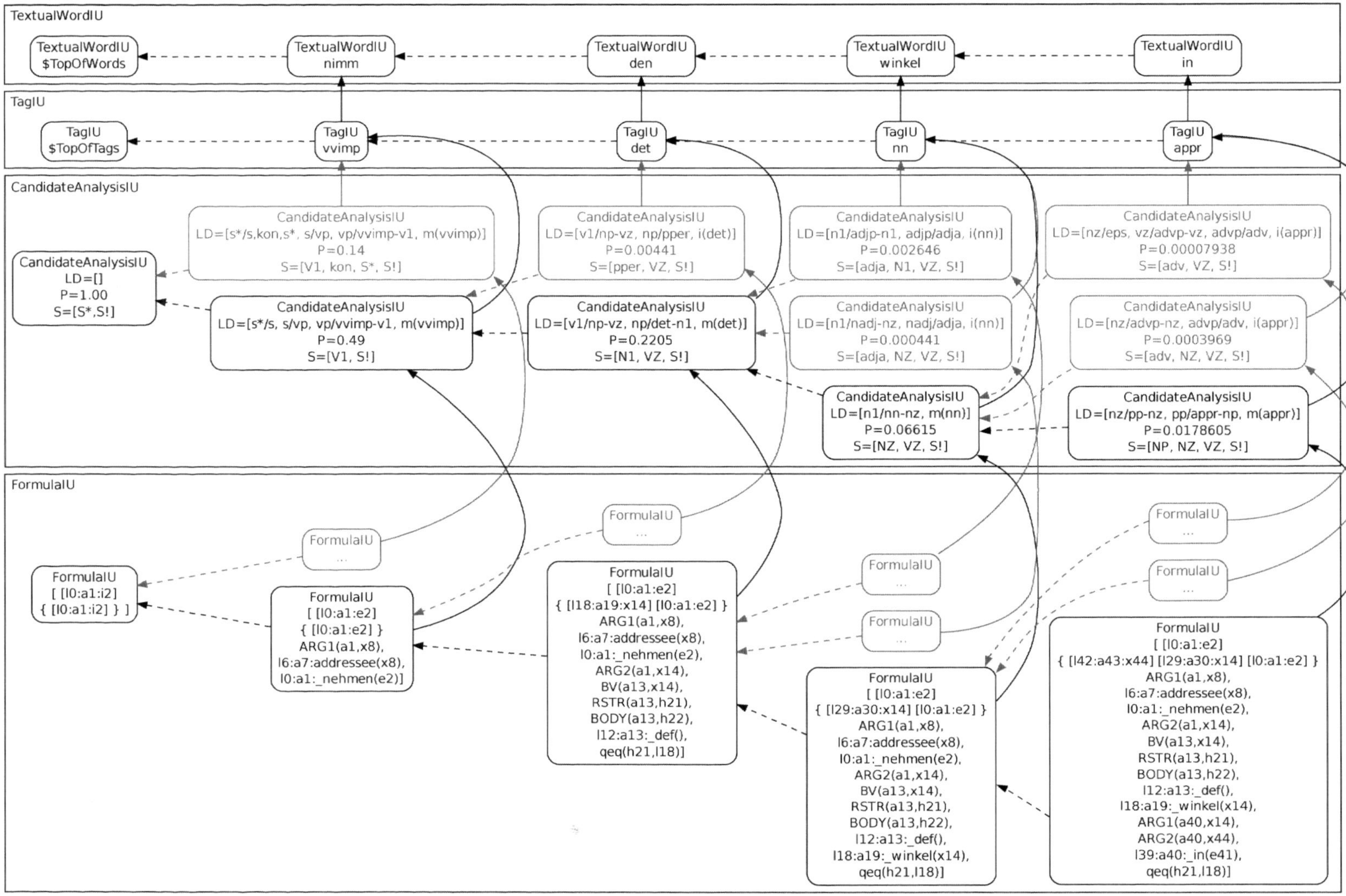

Figure 4: An example network of incremental units, including the levels of words, POS-tags, syntactic derivations and logical forms.

succeeding processing stages and newly incoming input. An illustration of such a network for our example sentence is shown in Figure 4. In our implementation, we assume IUs of the different processing stages: at the level of words (resulting from ASR or text input), of part-of-speech tags, of syntactic derivations and semantic representations. The different levels are arranged from top to bottom and unfold in time from left to right. Each level contains IUs of its type, shown as rounded boxes in the Figure. Dashed arrows link an IU to its predecessor on the same level. Multiple IUs sharing the same predecessor can be regarded as alternatives. Solid arrows indicate which information from a previous level an IU is grounded in (based on); here, every semantic IU is grounded in a syntactic IU, every syntactic IU in a POS-tag-IU, and so on.

Syntactic derivations ("CandidateAnalysisIUs") are represented by three features: a list of the last parser actions of the derivation (LD), with rule expansions or (robust) lexical matches; the derivation probability (P); and the remaining stack (S), where S* is the grammar's start symbol and S! an explicit end-of-input marker. (To keep the Figure small, we artificially reduced the beam size and cut off alternatives paths, shown in grey.) Semantic representations ("FormulaIUs") are shown by the resulting RMRS. Notice that, apart from the end-of-input marker, the stack of semantic slots (in curly brackets) is always synchronized with the parser's stack.

6 Using *i*RMRS for Dialogue Processing

Schlangen and Skantze (2009) have observed that incremental processing offers the potential not only to speed up responses of dialogue systems, but also to improve their processing, since "higher-level" results based on partial results from lower levels can be fed back to those lower levels and influence their further processing. In (Peldszus et al., 2012), we have shown how this can be realised using the framework detailed in the current paper. In that work, the semantic representations connected to each syntactic derivation—or, more specifically, those of referring expressions—were evaluated against the current dialogue environment in terms of their satisfiability. The result of this test was used as a signal that contributed to the weight of the current derivation and thus it had influence on the order of syntactic expansion. We could show a clear improvement of this processing style. In that work, we made use of the fact that our meaning representations can easily be simplified in a principled way, and used a simple rule-based reference resolution component.

In (Kennington and Schlangen, 2012), we then used our RMRS representations as input for a hybrid, probabilistic logic-based interpretation system, and showed that using these representations as input improved performance compared to a "words-only" model (as is often used in such statistical NLU work, as e.g. in (DeVault et al., 2011; Heintze et al., 2010)). In that work, we could directly transfer *i*RMRS predications into statements in the knowledge base over which the probabilistic reasoning was defined, where those statements could be combined freely with predicates describing the situational context.

These applications were made possible by the property of the framework described here to produce meaning representations at each input increment, which moreover can easily be transferred into shallower variants with loss of information (Peldszus et al., 2012) or into other first-order representation formats (Kennington and Schlangen, 2012). In current work, we are exploring more direct uses of the representations for discourse reasoning. The aim is to formulate discourse expectations, for example not only about the fact that an answer is expected after a question, but also that some aspects of its form can be predicted (for example, in an

NP question, the answer will, possibly implicitly, re-use the main predicate of the question) as *i*RMRS formulae. Annotating the syntactic top-down predictions with such discourse-based content expectations, and making use of the calculus for RMRS subsumption tests mentioned above (Copestake, 2007a), we have a principle mechanism at hand to let such expectations guide interpretation. We are currently evaluating whether this potential advantage translates into a practical improvement.

We cite these applications here as support for our claim that the representation format and construction mechanism described here can form the basis for a variety of work towards more flexible dialogue systems.

Conclusion

We have presented our approach to creating meaning representations for spontaneous spoken utterances. This approach is based on an existing, well-studied representation formalism, RMRS (Copestake, 2006) that can represent various levels of semantic detail, from shallow to deep; we have extended this to suit incremental construction, and so can create meaning representations in lockstep with incremental speech recognition (such as described in (Baumann et al., 2009)) feeding input to incremental parsing. We have described our implementation of such a parser and semantic construction component within an open framework for incremental processing, and have sketched some of the applications that we have already used this in.

While already fully functional within our domain, it remains for future work to extend coverage towards more general coverage. Here we plan to investigate using treebank resources to induce grammar and, the more challenging part, semantic macros for the grammar rules. Also, as sketched above, we are currently investigating using properties of the representation formalism (such as allowing for subsumption tests) to model top-down discourse expectations and evaluate their use for dialogue processing. After the first steps described in the present paper, the aim for that ongoing work is to bring us yet closer towards the goal of increasing both temporal and content-related flexibility of spoken dialogue systems.

Appendix

Definition 1 (Elementary predications). An elementary predication ℓ:a:$R(i)$ consists of a predicate symbol R, a label ℓ, an anchor a, and (optionally) as characteristic variable i an ordinary object language variable (i.e. an individual x, an event e or an underspecified index u).

Definition 2 (Argument relations). An argument relation $\mathsf{REL}(a, v)$ consists of an argument relation symbol REL from a finite set $\{\mathsf{ARG}_{\mathbb{N}}, \mathsf{BV}, \mathsf{RSTR}, \mathsf{BODY}, \mathsf{LEFT}_{i/\ell}, \mathsf{RIGHT}_{i/\ell}\}$, an anchor a, and exactly one argument v, which is either an ordinary object language variable $x/e/u$ or a hole h.

Definition 3 (RMRS structure under construction with a stack of slots). An RMRS structure under construction is a 6-tuple $\langle GT, H, S, R, C, E\rangle$,

- with GT the global top hole h_0,
- with H the hook $[\ell{:}a{:}i]$, consisting of the local top label ℓ, the anchor a and the index i,
- with S the stack of slots of the form $[\ell_n{:}a_n{:}i_n]$,
- with R the bag of elementary predications and argument relations,
- with C the bag of scope constraints and
- with E the set of variable equalities.

Definition 4 (Forward slot filling combination). Given two RMRSs, one being the functor $rmrs_f = \langle GT_f, H_f, S_f, R_f, C_f, E_f \rangle$ with the top slot $\text{top}(S_f) = [\ell_f{:}a_f{:}i_f]$ and one being the argument $rmrs_a = \langle GT_a, H_a, S_a, R_a, C_a, E_a \rangle$ with its hook $H_a = [\ell_a{:}a_a{:}i_a]$, the slot filling combination $rmrs_f \lhd rmrs_a$ yields an RMRS $rmrs = \langle GT, H, S, R, C, E \rangle$, s.t.

- $GT = GT_f = GT_a$
- $H = H_f$
- $S = \text{merge-stacks}(S_a, \text{pop}(S_f))$[2]
- $R = R_f \cup R_a$
- $C = C_f \cup C_a$
- $E = E_f \cup E_a \cup \{\ell_f = \ell_a, a_f = a_a, i_f = i_a\}$

A simple example of slot filling combination in a lexicalist setting

$$
\begin{array}{lll}
[[\textit{take}\ldots]] & = & [\ell_1{:}a_1{:}e_1]\ \{\,[\ell_3{:}a_3{:}x_3]\,\} \\
 & & \ell_1{:}a_1{:}\text{\_take\_v}(),\ \mathsf{ARG}_1(a_1,x_2),\ \mathsf{ARG}_2(a_1,x_3) \\
 & & \ell_2{:}a_2{:}\text{adressee}(x_2) \\
 & & \\
[[\textit{the}]] & = & [\ell_4{:}a_4{:}x_4]\ \{\,[\ell_5{:}a_5{:}x_4]\,\} \\
 & & \ell_4{:}a_4{:}\text{\_the\_q}(),\ \mathsf{BV}(a_4,x_4),\ \mathsf{RSTR}(a_4,h_1),\ \mathsf{BODY}(a_4,h_2),\ h_1 =_q \ell_5 \\
 & & \\
[[\textit{take}\ldots]] \lhd [[\textit{the}]] & = & [\ell_1{:}a_1{:}e_1]\ \{\,[\ell_5{:}a_5{:}x_4]\,\} \\
 & & \ell_1{:}a_1{:}\text{\_take\_v}(),\ \mathsf{ARG}_1(a_1,x_2),\ \mathsf{ARG}_2(a_1,x_3) \\
 & & \ell_2{:}a_2{:}\text{adressee}(x_2) \\
 & & \ell_4{:}a_4{:}\text{\_the\_q}(),\ \mathsf{BV}(a_4,x_4),\ \mathsf{RSTR}(a_4,h_1),\ \mathsf{BODY}(a_4,h_2),\ h_1 =_q \ell_5 \\
 & & \ell_3 = \ell_4,\ a_3 = a_4,\ x_3 = x_4 \\
 & & \\
 & = & [\ell_1{:}a_1{:}e_1]\ \{\,[\ell_5{:}a_5{:}x_3]\,\} \\
 & & \ell_1{:}a_1{:}\text{\_take\_v}(),\ \mathsf{ARG}_1(a_1,x_2),\ \mathsf{ARG}_2(a_1,x_3) \\
 & & \ell_2{:}a_2{:}\text{adressee}(x_2) \\
 & & \ell_3{:}a_3{:}\text{\_the\_q}(),\ \mathsf{BV}(a_3,x_3),\ \mathsf{RSTR}(a_3,h_1),\ \mathsf{BODY}(a_3,h_2),\ h_1 =_q \ell_5
\end{array}
$$

Some basic slotfilling combinators

$$
\begin{array}{lll}
[-] & = & [\ell{:}a{:}u]\ \{\,\}\,. \\
[\circ] & = & [\ell{:}a{:}u]\ \{\,[\ell{:}a{:}u]\,\}\,. \\
[=] & = & [\ell{:}a{:}u]\ \{\,[\ell{:}a{:}u][\ell{:}a{:}u]\,\}\,. \\
[+] & = & [\ell{:}a{:}u]\ \{\,[\ell_1{:}a_1{:}u][\ell{:}a{:}u]\,\}\,. \\
[+\!.] & = & [\ell{:}a{:}u]\ \{\,[\ell{:}a{:}u][\ell_1{:}a_1{:}u]\,\}\,. \\
[+\ell] & = & [\ell{:}a{:}u]\ \{\,[\ell{:}a_1{:}u][\ell{:}a{:}u]\,\}\,.
\end{array}
$$

Some of the semantic macros used in the grammar

$$
\begin{array}{llll}
[\text{Arg1}] & = & [\ell{:}a{:}u] & \{\,[\ell_1{:}a_1{:}x_1][\ell{:}a{:}u]\,\}\ \mathsf{ARG}_1(a,x_1) \\
[\text{Arg2}] & = & [\ell{:}a{:}u] & \{\,[\ell_1{:}a_1{:}x_1][\ell{:}a{:}u]\,\}\ \mathsf{ARG}_2(a,x_1) \\
[\text{Arg3}] & = & [\ell{:}a{:}u] & \{\,[\ell_1{:}a_1{:}x_1][\ell{:}a{:}u]\,\}\ \mathsf{ARG}_3(a,x_1) \\
[\text{adr}] & = & [\ell{:}a{:}x] & \{\,\}\ \ell{:}a{:}\text{addressee}(x) \\
[\text{Q}] & = & [\ell{:}a{:}x] & \{\,[\ell{:}a{:}e_1][\ell_2{:}a_2{:}x]\,\}\ \mathsf{BV}(a,x),\ \mathsf{RSTR}(a,h_1),\ \mathsf{BODY}(a,h_2),\ h_1 =_q \ell_2 \\
[\text{PP}] & = & [\ell{:}a{:}u] & \{\,[\ell_1{:}a_1{:}e_1][\ell_2{:}a_2{:}x_2]\,\}\ \mathsf{ARG}_1(a_1,u),\ \mathsf{ARG}_2(a_1,x_2) \\
[\text{Adj}] & = & [\ell{:}a{:}x] & \{\,[\ell{:}a_1{:}e_1]\,\}\ \mathsf{ARG}_1(a_1,x) \\
[\text{Adv}] & = & [\ell{:}a{:}u] & \{\,[\ell_1{:}a_1{:}e_1]\,\}\ \mathsf{ARG}_1(a_1,u) \\
[\text{Conj}] & = & [\ell{:}a{:}u] & \{\,[\ell_1{:}a_1{:}u_1][\ell{:}a{:}u][\ell_3{:}a_3{:}u_3]\,\}\ \mathsf{LEFT}_i(a,u_1),\ \mathsf{LEFT}_\ell(a,h_1), \\
 & & & \mathsf{RIGHT}_i(a,u_3),\ \mathsf{RIGHT}_\ell(a,h_3),\ h_1 =_q \ell_1,\ h_3 =_q \ell_3
\end{array}
$$

[2]The function merge-stacks(A,B) is understoods as yielding a new stack $S = \{a_1, \ldots, a_n, b_1, \ldots, b_n\}$ s.t. $a_1 = \text{top}(A)$ and $b_1 = \text{top}(B)$.

References

Aist, G., Allen, J., Campana, E., Gallo, C. G., Stoness, S., Swift, M., and Tanenhaus, M. K. (2007). Incremental understanding in human-computer dialogue and experimental evidence for advantages over nonincremental methods. In *Proceedings of Decalog 2007, the 11th International Workshop on the Semantics and Pragmatics of Dialogue*, Trento, Italy.

Allen, J., Manshadi, M., Dzikovska, M. O., and Swift, M. (2005). Deep linguistic processing for spoken dialogue systems. In *Proceedings of the 5th Workshop on Deep Linguistic Processing*, pages 49–56, Morristown, NJ, USA. Association for Computational Linguistics.

Allen, J. F., Shubert, L. K., Ferguson, G., Heeman, P., Hwang, C. H., Kato, T., Light, M., Martin, N. G., Miller, B. W., Poesio, M., and Traum, D. R. (1995). The TRAINS project: A case study in building a conversational planning agent. *Journal of Experimental and Theoretical AI*, 7:7–48.

Asher, N. and Lascarides, A. (2003). *Logics of Conversation*. Cambridge University Press, Cambridge.

Baumann, T., Atterer, M., and Schlangen, D. (2009). Assessing and improving the performance of speech recognition for incremental systems. In *Proceedings of the North American Chapter of the Association for Computational Linguistics - Human Language Technologies (NAACL HLT) 2009 Conference*, Boulder, Colorado, USA.

Baumann, T. and Schlangen, D. (2012). The InproTK 2012 release. In *Proceedings of the NAACL-HLT Workshop on Future directions and needs in the Spoken Dialog Community: Tools and Data (SDCTD 2012)*, pages 29–32, Montreal, Canada. ACL.

Bos, J. (1996). Predicate logic unplugged. In Dekker, P. and Stokhof, M., editors, *Proc. of the Tenth Amsterdam Colloquium*, pages 133–143, Amsterdam, Netherlands.

Briscoe, T. and Carroll, J. (2002). Robust accurate statistical annotation of general text. In *Proc. LREC*, pages 1499–1504.

Buß, O. and Schlangen, D. (2010). Modelling sub-utterance phenomena in spoken dialogue systems. In *Proceedings of the 14th International Workshop on the Semantics and Pragmatics of Dialogue (Pozdial 2010)*, pages 33–41, Poznan, Poland.

Clark, H. H. (1996). *Using Language*. Cambridge University Press, Cambridge.

Copestake, A. (2006). Robust minimal recursion semantics. Technical report, Cambridge Computer Lab. Unpublished draft.

Copestake, A. (2007a). *Invited Talk:* Applying Robust Semantics. In *Proceedings of PACLING 2007 – 10th Conference of the Pacific Association for Computational Linguistics*, pages 1–12, Melbourne.

Copestake, A. (2007b). Semantic composition with (robust) minimal recursion semantics. In *Proceedings of the Workshop on Deep Linguistic Processing*, DeepLP '07, pages 73–80, Stroudsburg, PA, USA. Association for Computational Linguistics.

Copestake, A., Flickinger, D., Pollard, C., and Sag, I. (2005). Minimal recursion semantics: An introduction. *Research on Language & Computation*, 3:281–332.

Deemter, K. v. and Peters, S., editors (1996). *Semantic Ambiguity and Underspecification*. CSLI, Stanford.

DeVault, D., Sagae, K., and Traum, D. (2011). Incremental Interpretation and Prediction of Utterance Meaning for Interactive Dialogue. *Dialogue and Discourse*, 2(1):143–170.

Domingos, P., Kok, S., Poon, H., Richardson, M., and Singla, P. (2006). Unifying logical and statistical AI. In *Proceedings of the Twenty-First National Conference on Artificial Intelligence*, pages 2–7, Boston, USA.

Ferguson, G. and Allen, J. F. (1998). TRIPS: An Integrated Intelligent Problem-Solving Assistant. In *Proceedings of the National Conference on Artificial Intelligence*, pages 567–573.

Fernández, R. and Schlangen, D. (2007). Referring under restricted interactivity conditions. In Keizer, S., Bunt, H., and Paek, T., editors, *Proceedings of the 8th SIGdial Workshop on Discourse and Dialogue*, pages 136–139, Antwerp, Belgium.

Flickinger, D. (2000). On building a more efficient grammar by exploiting types. *Natural Language Engineering*, 6(1):15–28.

Frege, G. (1897). Begriffsschrift – Eine der arithmetischen nachbildete Formalsprache des reines Denkens. Jena, Germany.

Gargett, A., Gregoromichelaki, E., Kempson, R., Purver, M., and Sato, Y. (2009). Grammar resources for modelling dialogue dynamically. *Cognitive Neurodynamics*, 3:347–363.

Heintze, S., Baumann, T., and Schlangen, D. (2010). Comparing local and sequential models for statistical incremental natural language understanding. In *Proc. SIGdial 2010*, pages 9–16, Tokyo, Japan.

Jurafsky, D. (2003). Pragmatics and computational linguistics. In Horn, L. R. and Wards, G., editors, *Handbook of Pragmatics*. Blackwell, Oxford, UK.

Kempson, R., Meyer-Viol, W., and Gabbay, D. (2001). *Dynamic syntax: the flow of language understanding*. Blackwell.

Kennington, C. and Schlangen, D. (2012). Markov logic networks for situated incremental natural language understanding. In *Proceedings of the SIGdial Conference 2012*, Seoul, South Korea.

Koller, A. and Lascarides, A. (2009). A logic of semantic representations for shallow parsing. In *Proc. EACL 2009*, pages 451–459, Athens.

Peldszus, A., Buß, O., Baumann, T., and Schlangen, D. (2012). Joint satisfaction of syntactic and pragmatic constraints improves incremental spoken language understanding. In *Proceedings of the 13th Conference of the European Chapter of the Association for Computational Linguistics*, pages 514–523, Avignon, France. Association for Computational Linguistics.

Pinkal, M. (1996). Radical underspecification. In Dekker, P., Groenendijk, J., and Stokhoff, M., editors, *Proceedings of the 10th Amsterdam Colloqium*, Amsterdam.

Poesio, M. and Rieser, H. (2010). Completions, coordination, and alignment in dialogue. *Dialogue and Discourse*, 1(1):1–89.

Poesio, M. and Traum, D. (1997). Conversational actions and discourse situations. *Computational Intelligence*, 13(3):309–347.

Purver, M., Eshghi, A., and Hough, J. (2011). Incremental semantic construction in a dialogue system. In Bos, J. and Pulman, S., editors, *Proceedings of the 9th International Conference on Computational Semantics (IWCS)*, pages 365–369, Oxford, UK.

Reyle, U. (1993). Dealing with ambiguities by underspecification: Construction, representation and deduction. *Journal of Semantics*, 10:123–179.

Roark, B. E. (2001). *Robust Probabilistic Predictive Syntactic Processing: Motivations, Models, and Applications*. PhD thesis, Department of Cognitive and Linguistic Sciences, Brown University.

Sagae, K., Christian, G., DeVault, D., and Traum, D. (2009). Towards natural language understanding of partial speech recognition results in dialogue systems. In *Short paper Proc. NAACL-HLT'09)*, Boulder, Colorado, USA.

Schäfer, U. (2007). *Integrating Deep and Shallow Natural Language Processing Components – Representations and Hybrid Architectures*. PhD thesis, Faculty of Mathematics and Computer Science, Saarland University, Saarbrücken, Germany.

Schlangen, D. (2003). *A Coherence-Based Approach to the Interpretation of Non-Sentential Utterances in Dialogue*. PhD thesis, School of Informatics, University of Edinburgh, Edinburgh, UK.

Schlangen, D., Baumann, T., and Atterer, M. (2009). Incremental reference resolution: The task, metrics for evaluation, and a bayesian filtering model that is sensitive to disfluencies. In *Proceedings of SIGdial 2009, the 10th Annual SIGDIAL Meeting on Discourse and Dialogue*, London, UK.

Schlangen, D. and Lascarides, A. (2003). The interpretation of non-sentential utterances in dialogue. In Rudnicky, A., editor, *Proceedings of the 4th SIGdial workshop on Discourse and Dialogue*, Sapporo, Japan.

Schlangen, D. and Skantze, G. (2009). A general, abstract model of incremental dialogue processing. In *EACL '09: Proceedings of the 12th Conference of the European Chapter of the Association for Computational Linguistics*, pages 710–718. Association for Computational Linguistics.

Skantze, G. and Hjalmarsson, A. (2010). Towards incremental speech generation in dialogue systems. In *Proceedings of the SIGdial 2010 Conference*, pages 1–8, Tokyo, Japan.

Skantze, G. and Schlangen, D. (2009). Incremental dialogue processing in a micro-domain. In *Proceedings of the 12th Conference of the European Chapter of the Association for Computational Linguistics (EACL 2009)*, Athens, Greece.

Steedman, M. (2000). *The Syntactic Process*. MIT Press, Cambridge, Massachusetts.

Zettlemoyer, L. S., Milch, B., and Kealbling, L. P. (2009). Multi-agent filtering with infinitely nested beliefs. In *Neural Information Processing Systems (NIPS)*.

Abstracts of Invited Position Papers

Remarks on some not so closed issues concerning discourse connectives

Aravind Joshi
University of Pennsylvania, USA

ABSTRACT

By now, we have quite a bit of data about discourse connectives as they manifest themselves in various types of corpora in a few languages. It is quite remarkable that many aspects of these connectives are quite stable across languages. However, as has been observed already, the class of these connectives in not quite a closed class. I will briefly comment on this partially open nature of this class. I will also briefly (and perhaps wildly) speculate what we might learn by looking at other modalities of linguistic communication.

Penn Discourse Treebank Relations and their Potential for Language Generation

Kathleen McKeown
Columbia University, USA

ABSTRACT

In the early eighties, language generation researchers explored the use of rhetorical relations, in the form of schemata or common patterns of rhetorical structure (McKeown 1985) and later in the form of rhetorical structure theory (RST) (Mann 1984). Researchers in language generation showed how discourse structure could be used to plan the content of a text (McKeown 1985, Moore and Paris 1993, Hovy 1988). In most cases, structure was linked in some way to content, whether directly or through planning how to satisfy speaker intentions, and this was critical to the success of using discourse structure for content planning. Later work (Barzilay 2010, Barzilay and Lapata 2005) took a modern approach to this problem, developing techniques to learn common discourse structures for specific domains and using these learned discourse structures to control content selection and organization.

In this panel discussion, I will address questions about how the Penn Discourse Treebank could be used for generation or summarization.

Using PDTB relations for determining content in text summarization has recently been addressed by Louis et al (Louis et al. 2010). While they found that discourse structure was a strong indicator for determining salience for text summaries, they also found that lexical overlap performed equally well at determining salience and was easier to compute. This is a topic that could use further exploration. Could further research on the use of PDTB relations improve their performance to surpass the use of lexical indicators? Lexical indicators have been used for years in summarization and it would be somehow more satisfactory if other factors could be shown to play an important role. Could PDTB relations be used in conjunction with abstractive methods more effectively than extractive methods?

In language generation, discourse structure relations often play a prescriptive role in determining what to say next. If content has already been selected, that content in conjunction with discourse structure can be used to constrain what gets said next. PDTB relations have been empirically determined through analysis of text and there has been an effort to limit the range of relations. One natural question is whether PDTB relations should serve the same role as RST in generating of text or whether there is a difference in how they could be applied. Could the specific annotation of senses associated with relations be used to help determine content? There is an aspect of the PDTB which differs from earlier work on RST as it ties in closer to the syntactic structure of the text. Could the close coupling of discourse structure, syntactic structure and sense annotation offer an advantage over previous methods? One possibility would be to explore the role it could play in sentence planning, the problem of determining how to combine simple propositions to generate more complex sentences.

References

Barzilay, R. 2010. Probabilistic Approaches for Modeling Text Structure and Their Application to Text-to-Text Generation. In Emiel Krahmer and Mariet Theune, editors, *Empirical Methods in Natural Language Generation: Data-oriented Methods and Empirical Evaluation,* Springer.

Barzilay, R., and Lapata, M. 2005. Collective Content Selection for Concept-To-Text Generation. In *Proceedings of EMNLP 2005*.

Hovy, E. 1988. Planning coherent multisentential text. In *Proceedings of the 26th annual meeting on Association for Computational Linguistics,* pp. 163-169.

Louis, A., and Nenkova, A. 2012. A coherence model based on syntactic patterns. In *Proceedings of EMNLP-CoNLL 2012*.

Mann, B. 1984. Discourse structures for text generation. In *Proceedings of the 10th International Conference on Computational Linguistics and 22nd annual meeting of Association for Computational Linguistics,* Stroudsburg, PA, pp. 367-375.

McKeown, K. R. 1985. *Text Generation: Using Discourse Strategies and Focus Constraints to Generate Natural Language Text.* Cambridge University Press, Cambridge, England, 1985.

Moore, J., and Paris, C. 1993. Planning text for advisory dialogues: capturing intentional and rhetorical information. In *Journal Computational Linguistics, Volume 19 Issue 4,* December 1993, pp. 651-694.

New Information in Wikitalk - story telling for information presentation

Kristiina Jokinen
University of Helsinki, Finland
University of Tartu, Estonia

ABSTRACT

In this talk I will discuss issues related to information presentation in an interactive system, Wikitalk (Wilcock & Jokinen, 2011). This supports open-domain conversations using Wikipedia as a knowledge base, and it has been implemented on Nao a spoken dialogue system. The novel feature in the system is that by extending the robot's interaction capabilities by enabling Nao to talk about an unlimited range of topics.

I will focus especially on how to present new information in a manner that allows the user to follow the presentation. The user can query Wikipedia via the Nao robot and have chosen entries read out by the robot. In a text-free environment the user needs to infer the structure of the article from the robot's output - Wikipedia entries are large blocks of text which can be very monotonous when simply read out by a synthetic voice, and comprehension could be enhanced by adding non-verbal cues to discourse level organization of the text. In Wikipedia relevant information is marked with hyperlinks to other entries. A system where the robot could signal these links non-verbally while reading the text would allow the user to further query the encyclopedia without recourse to explicit menus.

The articles are considered as possible Topics that the robot can talk about, while each link in the article is treated as new information that the user can shift their attention to, and ask for more information. The paragraphs and sentences in the article are considered as propositional chunks, i.e. pieces of information that structure the topic into subtopics and form the minimal units for presentation, i.e. they can be presented in one 'utterance' by the robot.

The challenge in presenting the Wikipedia information is how to convey its structure to the user so that she can understand which are the new information links, and how to navigate in the topic structure smoothly. In dialogue management, topics are usually managed by a stack, which allows a convenient last-in-first-out mechanism to handle topics that have been recently talked about. We use topic trees (cf. McCoy and Cheng 1990, Jokinen et al. 1996) in which topics are structured into a tree that enables more flexible management of the recent topics.

Moreover, we use the concepts of Topic and NewInfo (Jokinen 2009) where Topic refers to the particular issue (Wiki-article) that the speakers are talking about, and NewInfo is the part of the message that is new in the context of the current Topic (links). It must be emphasized that the dialogue coherence, i.e. the relation between consecutive utterances being such that the listener can readily understand what their connection is, appears straightforward: we can rely on the structure of the Wikipedia to provide coherence for us. As the Wikipedia articles have already been written so that they form a coherent text, we take advantage of this and assume that the content of the topics and possible NewInfo links is coherent. Meaningfulness of the interaction is based on the user's interest rather than a particular task structure that would limit the suitable topics for the interaction.

However, what is important in our case is to capture the speakers' attentional state in such a way that the user can focus their attention to NewInfo. We have experimented with various gestures to mark the NewInfo and to provide structuring for the WikiTalk presentation. Gesture and posture changes could also be used to help manage turntaking in Nao's dialogue, while the inclusion of gesture in Nao's conversational repertoire would also enhance expressivity and add liveliness to the interaction. We identified a set of gestures which could be used to:

- mark discourse level details such as paragraph and sentence boundaries,
- indicate hyperlinks,
- help manage turntaking,
- add expressivity or liveliness.

Empirical methods in the study of anaphora: lessons learned, remaining problems

Massimo Poesio
University of Essex, UK

ABSTRACT

In the last ten years we witnessed the creation of anaphorically annotated corpora[1] of substantial size (between 500,000 and 1 million tokens) and for many languages, including Arabic, Catalan, Chinese, Czech, Dutch, English, German, Italian, Japanese, and Spanish. These resources have enabled a flourishing of evaluation initiatives devoted to the cross-lingual computational study of anaphora, such as SEMEVAL-2010, the CONLL 2011 shared task, and now the CONLL 2012 shared task (Arabic, Chinese and English). The results obtained in such campaigns indicate, however, that there is still a way to go before this task is understood to the degree of other aspects of natural language interpretation, including tasks such as semantic role labelling. In this talk I will discuss the lessons learned during our experience with the annotation of the GNOME and ARRAU corpora of English, the LiveMemories corpus of Italian, and the ongoing annotation using the Phrase Detective game[2] and the issues that still remain to be tackled.

1 I will use the term 'anaphora' to refer to the linguistic task as defined, say, in Discourse Representation Theory, in contrast with the 'coreference' task in the sense of ACE and MUC.

2 http://www.phrasedetectives.org

Explicit and implicit discourse relations from a cross-lingual perspective – from experience in working on Chinese discourse annotation

Nianwen (Bert) Xue
Brandeis University, USA

ABSTRACT

In the field of computational linguistics or natural language processing, progress in discourse analysis has been relatively slow, as compared with syntactic parsing or semantic analysis (e.g., word sense disambiguation, semantic role labeling). In this age when statistical, data-driven approaches dominate the field, having a common linguistic resource that is widely accepted by the community is key to advancing the state of the art in this area. To create consistently annotated data for discourse analysis is particularly challenging because one has to deal with larger linguistic structures and there are few linguistic rules to follow. The key to successful discourse annotation is to identify a well-grounded linguistic theory that can be easily operationalized. In the Penn Discourse Treebank (Prasad et al. 2008, Webber and Joshi 1998) the field may have found such a theory. In the PDTB conception, discourse relations revolve around discourse connectives, where each discourse connective is a predicate that takes two arguments. In this way, discourse annotations are anchored by discourse connectives and are thus lexicalized. In our view, lexicalization has been crucial to the success of the PDTB as an annotation project, a large-scale effort characterized by high inter-annotator agreement, a standard metric for annotation consistency. Lexicalization makes highly abstract discourse relations grounded to a specific lexical item. In doing so, it localizes the ambiguity in discourse relations to discourse connectives, where a lexical item can have either a discourse connective use or a non-discourse connective use (e.g., ``when"), and one discourse connective can be ambiguous between different discourse relations (e.g., ``since"). As a result, it reduces the cognitive load of the annotation task because each annotator can focus on only one discourse connective at a time instead of scores of discourse relations. This in turn enlarges the annotator pool and more annotators will be able to perform the task without having to have extensive training. The long list of annotators who worked on the PDTB annotation attests to this observation. A larger annotator pool and a shorter learning curve translates to the scalability of such an approach.

If lexicalization is so important to discourse annotation, what about discourse relations that are not anchored by an explicit discourse connective? The PDTB addresses this by assuming there is an *implicit* discourse connective that connects its two arguments, which are typically (parts of) adjacent sentences. This is operationalized by identifying punctuation marks (e.g., periods) that serve as boundaries of two adjacent sentences as anchors of implicit discourse relations. The specific discourse relation is determined by testing which discourse connective can be plausibly inserted between these two adjacent sentences. In doing so, the PDTB assumes that (1) the range of possible discourse relations anchored by implicit discourse connectives are basically the same as those anchored by explicit discourse relations, and (2) discourse relations anchored by implicit discourse connectives are mostly local. The first assumption is largely born out in the PDTB. Either a discourse connective can be inserted between two adjacent sentences, or they are related by the fact that they talk about the same entities, or there is no relation between them. The last possibility has a direct bearing on the second question: if there is no relation between two adjacent sentences, does that mean that these sentences have no discourse relations at all with the rest of the text, or that they are related to other discourse segments that are non-local? It is reasonable to assume that all discourse segments are related in a coherent piece of text, and large number of such "no-relations" would call for a significant expansion to the PDTB approach.

While it might not be too much to expect that the same high-level discourse relations hold across languages, it is almost certainly too much to expect that discourse relations are lexicalized in the same way across languages. The question is whether a lexicalized approach to discourse analysis can still be maintained in languages where discourse relations are lexicalized in ways that are significantly different from English . Our experience in a pilot PDTB-style Chinese discourse annotation project shows that the lexicalized approach can be effectively adopted, although significant adaptations have to be made. Chinese has the same types of discourse connectives (subordinate conjunctions, coordinate conjunctions, and discourse adverbials) as English, but they occur much less frequently because they can often be dropped. The ratio of implicit and explicit connectives is about 80/20 (Zhou and Xue, 2012) rather than the roughly 50/50 split reported for PDTB (Prasad et al 2008). However, by identifying punctuation marks as boundaries of discourse segments and test whether lexicalized discourse relations hold between adjacent comma-separated discourse segments, we are able to show that Chinese discourse annotation can be performed with very good consistency. More evidence has to be gathered from the experience of other languages to test the feasibility of lexicalized approaches to discourse annotation in a multi-lingual setting, and such evidence will come soon now that such an approach has been adopted in a number of discourse annotation projects for a variety of different languages.

References

Webber, B., and Joshi, A. 1998. Anchoring a Lexicalized Tree-Adjoining grammar for Discourse. In *Proceedings of ACL/COLING Workshop on Discourse Relations and Discourse Markers,* Montreal, Canada, August 1998.

Prasad, R., Dinesh, N., Lee, A., Miltsakaki, E., Robaldo, L., Joshi, A., and Webber, B. 2010. The Penn Discourse Treebank 2.0. In *Proceedings of the 6th International Conference on Language Resources and Evaluation (LREC 2008).* Marrakech, Morocco, June 2008.

Zhou, Y., and Xue, N. 2012. PDTB-style discourse annotation of Chinese text. In *Proceedings of ACL-2012.* Jeju Island, Korea.

Author Index

Association for Computational Linguistics
209 N. Eighth Street
Stroudsburg, Pennsylvania 18360